FINDING
EACH OTHER IN
JUDAISM

MEDITATIONS ON THE

RITES OF PASSAGE FROM

BIRTH TO IMMORTALITY

HAROLD M. SCHULWEIS

ARTWORK BY JEANETTE KUVIN OREN

UAHC PRESS · NEW YORK

Library of Congress Cataloging-in-Publication Data

Schulweis, Harold M.

Finding each other in Judaism : meditations on the rites of passage from birth to immortality / by Harold M. Schulweis.

p. cm.

ISBN 0-8074-0764-X (pbk. : alk. paper)

1. Judaism—Customs and practices—Meditations. 2. Life cycle, Human—Religious aspects—Judaism—Meditations. 3. Life change events—Religious aspects—Judaism—Meditations. 4. Jewish meditations. 5. Life cycle, Human—Religious aspects—Judaism—Poetry. I. Title.

BM700.S345 2001

296.4'4—dc21   00-054503

Dedicated to Malkah.

My gratitude for the editorial counsel of Rabbi Hara Person whose surname translates her mentshlicheit and erudition. I would also like to thank the other members of the UAHC Press who worked with dedication on this book: Ken Gesser, Stuart Benick, Rick Abrams, Debra Hirsch Corman, Liane Broido, and Eric Eisenkramer.

My friend and secretary Ms. Karen Cothren has been more than a spell check in assiduously reading and typing this manuscript.

I have been privileged to share the rites of passage of my Valley Beth Shalom congregants who motivated the writing of this book.

Harold M. Schulweis

CONTENTS

Each individual must first find himself within himself, then he must also find himself in the world about himself; his society, his community, his nation. The community must find itself within itself; then it must find itself in all of humanity.

Humanity must first find itself within itself; then it must find itself in the world.

The world must find itself within itself; then it must find itself within the universe that surrounds it.

The surrounding universe in its generality must first find itself within itself; then it must find itself in the highest category of universality.

Universality must first find itself within itself; then it must find itself in the fullness that fills, in the highest light, in the hub of life, in the divine light.

Abraham Isaac Kook, Orot HaKodesh II

WHY THIS BOOK?

Overcoming Riteless Passages
and Passageless Rites

I have always been taken by the Jewish folktale that wonders why God created the human being and why on the sixth day, so late in the order of Creation. Was the decision an afterthought? The folktale explains that, despite the plenitude of creatures created during the first five days, God was lonely. Yearning for companionship, God created the human being in God's own Image and likeness (Genesis 1:27). Out of personal experience with God's latest creation came a divine wisdom that reverberates throughout the Jewish tradition: "It is not good that the human being should be alone" (Genesis 2:18). A helpmate is created in the Image of God, a human companion with whom the first human being can find himself. For the self is discovered not in isolation, on a desert island or mountaintop, but in relationship with an other. The search to discover *who* I am leads to the quest to discover *whose* I am.

Following the Book of Genesis, the nucleus of two persons is the foundation of the family whose patriarchs and matriarchs form a people in whom "all the families of the earth shall be blessed" (Genesis 12:3). Family becomes the matrix out of which civilization originates and develops. The sacred glue of the family *(mishpachah)* promises to knit together the isolated and lonely beings of Creation. Today, there is a growing consensus that the binding powers of the family do not hold and that ways must be found to strengthen the disconnected bonds.

I have been moved by the cry of Franz Kafka, who bemoaned his tragic alienation from his father and imagined how things could have been different. Addressing his father, Franz wrote: "We might both have found each other in Judaism" (*Kafka versus Kafka,* 1968). Like Kafka, we need to give thought to the squandered opportunities to transform the family through the shared values of Jewish spirit and purpose. Such opportunities are especially afforded us during the rites of passage.

A child is born, a wedding is in the offing, a death is pending. The family is gathered, and something must be done, something must be said. These are the emotionally charged moments when it is not good for us to be alone and not good enough to offer a handshake, a cigar, a card announcing name, height, and weight. On such occasions, even those most distanced from Jewish community and tradition seek out a synagogue or rabbi, sensing the tug of an invisible cord, a tie to "obscure forces and emotions, all the more powerful the less they were to be defined in words" (*The Complete Work of Sigmund Freud,* 1959). In the same way, a secular Jew like the American philosopher Morris Raphael Cohen, who thoroughly repudiated supernaturalism, singled out for appreciation "the ancient ceremonies that celebrate the coming and going of life, the wedding ceremony, the birth and burial services which give an expression to the continuity of the spiritual tradition that is more eloquent than any phrase of my own creation" (*A Dreamer's Journey,* 1949). We seek a community that shares the sanctity of these events, commemorating them with a meaningful choreography.

Beyond the public festivals and fasts of Judaism, it is in the private domain of rites of passage that make up the stages of our lives that we find deepened and broadened relationships. Through the rites of passage, the "I" draws closer to the "we," to the members of the family, and to the community present and past. These singular intersections present unique circumstances in which to find one other in Judaism. Laughter and tears crave community.

Riteless Passages and Passageless Rites

There are two obstacles that dissipate the potentiality of bringing the family closer through Judaism: riteless passages and passageless rites. By riteless passages I mean the secular marking of life's stages without ritual anchoring, religious meaning, or spiritual reflection. Events simply transpire in calendrical time. They are treated as purely private occasions, free of the constraints of communal traditions. Ceremony is regarded as extraneous: so a birth without benediction, a wedding without sanctifying rituals, a funeral without *Kaddish*.

But riteless passages create their own vacuum. I recall an intense conversation with a secularly sophisticated man whose father had just died. He explained himself as neither religious nor unbelieving. He wanted my "services," the simplest ceremony without, as he put it, "ritual complexity." Toward the end of the conversation, he stopped to ask, "Now, tell me how to mourn." It was said in all seriousness. When I questioned what he meant, he explained that he wanted to mourn in a way that his father would recognize. He wanted to mourn in a way that would bind him to his father through the familiar sounds of prayer. He sensed that in some important way, his father's immortality was bound up with the presence of a Jewish community. Later, after the funeral and after the mourning period, he told me what the presence of the minyan, the ten Jewish persons whose presence is needed for prayers during the seven days of mourning, had meant to him. For among the members of the minyan were members of his family, many of whom he had not seen for many years. Their presence gave him comfort; even after the radical disconnection of death, he was connected in another significant way. Riteless passages deny us that opportunity to discover the profound spiritual implications of life-altering events.

The second obstacle that stands in the way of finding each other is the phenomenon of passageless rites. Here pro forma ceremonies take place; ritual is observed but in a manner that desacralizes. In the same letter to his father, Franz Kafka recalls the ritual emptiness that further estranged him: "Later, as a boy, I could not understand how, with the insignificant scrap of Judaism you yourself possessed, you could reproach me for not . . . making an effort to cling to a similar insignificant scrap" (*Kafka versus Kafka*, 1968). His reaction was not atypical. His reference to the farcical conduct of the Passover seder at home is reminiscent of the report by his contemporary, the philosopher Franz Rosenzweig. The Passover seder simply was abolished in Rosenzweig's home because his uncles ridiculed the mumbled recitation of the Haggadah. Gershom Scholem, the great contemporary scholar of Jewish mysticism, recalls with embarrassment the trivialization of ritual by his father, who would light his cigar from the Sabbath lights and recite a mock Hebrew benediction over tobacco.

Passageless rites convert the covenantal *b'rit* ceremony into a surgical procedure; the bar or bat mitzvah into a birthday party; the wedding into a ceremony centered around the caterer's menu, the florist's display, and the photographer's angles; the divorce into a mechanical dissolution of a contract; and the funeral into a black-bordered obituary announcing the time and place of the disposal of the body. "Ceremony" has entered our vocabulary as a definition of boredom and irrelevance. *Webster's Third International Dictionary* defines a ceremony as "an action performed with formality but lacking deep significance, form, or effect." The opportunity for the transmission of the wisdom and poetry of Judaism and, with it, the chance to connect as a family is squandered, and in its place emerges the kind of perfunctory performance against which the prophet Isaiah inveighed: "Because that people has approached Me with its mouth and honored Me with the lips, but has kept their heart far from Me, and its worship of Me has become a commandment of men learned by rote, truly I shall further baffle that people with bafflement upon bafflement, and the wisdom of its wise shall fail, and the prudence of its prudent shall vanish" (Isaiah 29:13–14). For many today, the rituals of life passage are experienced merely as prescriptions and proscriptions bereft of the grace and wisdom of rationale. The myths and poetry, ethics and philosophy of a civilization that underlie the rites of passage are buried beneath the arid sands of ritual routine.

Overcoming the Disconnection

The critique of riteless passages and passageless rites reveals a dangerous chasm at the heart of Jewish life. It involves a disjunction that separates behavior from belief, ritual from rationale, performance from philosophy. This split in thinking threatens the richness of the rite of passage and undermines its potential for uniting the family through Jewish practice.

The tendency to separate an act from its meaningful purpose has a long history. It is based on the biblical record of the Jews who heard the words of God at Sinai and responded, *"Naaseh v'nishma"*—"We will do and we will hear" (Exodus 24:7). This wording is taken to legitimate the primacy of doing over understanding, of performing over explaining, with the implication that meaning will eventually follow. But too often that never happens. The choice between behavior and meaning remains frozen in an either/or disjunction. So formulated, religious instruction tends to follow two diverse paths. Do you believe what you do, or do you do what you believe? Do you feel what you do, or do you do what you feel? The behaviorists focus mainly upon ritual performance, concentrating on the how, where, and when a ritual is performed. Those who focus on the meaning and purpose behind performance dwell on the questions of why and what for.

Taken separately, each has its strengths and weaknesses. The ritual behaviorist externalizes his Jewish identity with concrete actions, the fluency of the words of prayers, and the logistics of ritual motion. He or she knows "how," but little of the spiritual significance. On the other hand, the rationale seekers are often so engaged in the theoretic meaning of the rites that they end up talking about prayer, talking about the ritual, talking about the Festivals. Such an approach yields a meta-Judaism, an "about-ism" that talks of the essence of Jewish living but weakens the observance that sustains it. Orthopraxy has the virtues of discipline and structure. Theology offers the motivation and rationale that elevate the ritual beyond the routine gesture. But practice without theory is blind, and theory without practice is empty. Either/or rends the organic unity of head, heart, and hand. Consequently, many of us fall between the tables, wanting more spiritual nourishment but not knowing how to achieve it.

In this book I have sought to bridge the chasm, to properly hyphenate rite and passage, to connect behaving with believing, doing with under-standing. The book opens each section of the rites of passage with rabbinic and philosophic interpretation, folkloristic parables and insights. These point to the theological rationale and the ethical implications of the rites of passage. The prose introductions are followed by poetic and reflective meditations I have composed that may be incorporated in the life-cycle celebrations. The task is to repair the rupture between act and purpose, between the private and the communal, between the unique and the universal and, in so doing, enable the participants to find themselves and each other in a larger Jewish life.

Holding On and Letting Go

To follow the rites of passage from birth to death is to trace the route of the self's spiritual career as it grows from one stage of life to another. From the covenant at birth to the first day at school, from the moral autonomy marked by the bar/bat mitzvah to the biblical counsel to marry and leave the parents and cleave to one's spouse, from the cutting of the fringes of the prayer shawl laid upon the body of the deceased at the funeral to prayers of remembrance at *Yizkor,* the journey of transitions and transformations of a life are brought to awareness, refining and deepening the sense of the sacred underlying all of them.

Each transition helps us come to terms with the dual wisdom of letting go and holding on. In every rite, some ties are loosened to free us for further attachments. As celebrants, we are like aerialists on a swinging trapeze, letting go of one ring to catch hold of another. Something old is loosened and something new is discovered in the transformations that are marked through the rites of passage. At my bar/bat mitzvah, I am no longer a child. I have assumed new responsibilities and obligations that I did not own before. At my wedding, I transform my syntax from "I" and "mine" to "we" and "ours." At my death, I am no longer obligated to perform mitzvot. I am dependent upon others for the continuity of my memory.

The Image Within

In each of the markers of the transition and transformation, what is constant? What is the unsevered cord that provides the continuity between one stage and another? The fixed referent that runs through all of the rites of passage is found in the root principle called in Hebrew *Tzelem Elohim,* the divine Image. It is introduced in the biblical account of the creation of the human being and is elaborated in rabbinic thought: "And God created man in His image, in the image of God created He him; male and female created He them" (Genesis 1:27). The Image of God within is the root metaphor that captures the unique Jewish understanding of the human self, its inner life, and its profound relations with God and humanity. In the biblical account, the human being has a special status and responsibility. All other creatures God formed by God's word, except the human being, whom God created through God's own acts: "The Lord God formed Adam from the dust of the earth. He blew into his nostrils the breath of life, and man became a living being" (Genesis 2:7).

The *Tzelem Elohim* signifies both the uniqueness and universality of the human soul. While no man is a clone of another, all human beings, regardless of race or religion, are born imprinted with the Image of the Imageless God. The powers of the Image within are variously named: soul, spirit, breath, intellect, will, conscience. Every child enters the world stamped by the divine Image.

But the Image of God is not a sealed package. People were created with the capacity "to become" what the Image of God implies: the cultivation of the sacred potential within the depths of their rational and emotional moral being. The Image is an aspiration, a resemblance rather than an identity with God. The actualization of the Image is a never-ending process, coterminous with life itself, a work in progress from the first to the last breath of human life. The appreciation, cultivation, and refinement of the Image of God is the spiritual subtext of the rites of passage. The liturgy and ritual drama expressed in these rites commit and recommit us to this evolution.

Imitation of Godliness

In Judaism, the essential test for us as human beings is living our lives in a way that makes manifest the attributes of godliness. But as one rabbinic Sage asks, how is it possible for a fallible, mortal human being to fulfill the mandate to walk in God's way, seeing that God is described as "a devouring fire" (Deuteronomy 4:24). How can the finite soul emulate the mysterious essence of divinity?

It is not the face but the back of God that is imitated. It is not the penetration of the secrets of God's essence that is the goal, but the observed consequences of God's moral behavior that is the path to be sought. God informed Moses, "I will take away My hand and you shall see My back, but My face you shall not see" (Exodus 33:23). God is Imageless, but God's ways are discernible and emulatable.

God made for Adam and Eve coats of skin and clothed them. As God clothed the naked, so do thou. God visited Abraham when he was ailing at the oak of Mamre. As God visited the sick, do thou also. God comforted Isaac after the death of Abraham. As God comforted the bereaved, do thou also. God buried Moses in the valley. As God attended to the deceased, do thou also (Talmud, *Sotah* 14a).

God is verified, made true *(veri-facere)*, in our lives not by syllogistic argument or the declaration of dogmas, but by acting out the accessible attributes of divinity. The gift of *Imago Dei,* the Image of God, pulls us toward *imitatio Dei,* the lived imitation of God. Belief in God's reality and goodness is behaved.

The Image of God, shadowed in the human being, implies a special closeness with God, a unique human collegiality with the Divine. Acknowledging the gift of the Image, the human being is elevated as a partner with God in sustaining and transforming the self and its environment. The internalized Image bears testimony to the divine-human resemblance, a shared moral affinity. To become aware of the ideal Image of divinity within is to become conscious of human power and human responsibility. The prophet Isaiah acknowledges that divine-human kinship when he cites God's address to the people: "Ye are My witnesses saith the Lord" (Isaiah 43:10). The Rabbis translate God's claim conditionally, "If ye are My witnesses I am the Lord, and if ye are not My witnesses I am, as it were, not the Lord" (*Sifrei D'varim* 33:5). Herein lies a Jewish theology of human self-esteem, a self-respect gained not by self-aggrandizement but by the self's aspiration toward godliness. A theology of self in a community of shared values resides in the strands of each and every rite of passage.

The Jewish insistence on the interdependence of divinity and humanity encourages the creative involvement of the self in God's universe. Consider the passage in Genesis 2:5 wherein we are told that in the beginning there was no shrub or herb in the field because "God had not yet caused it to rain upon the earth and there was no human to till the soil." The connection between the falling rain from heaven and the human tilling of the earth symbolizes the significance of human-divine interdependence. The biblical verse describes the transaction between the given from above and the transformation from below. Where there is no action emanating from below, there is no action emanating from above. It is only when the human being prepares the earth beneath that a mist rises up from the earth, watering the face of the earth. So it is that partnership with God carries profound theological implications for the prayers and benedictions that surround the rites of passage. For example, focusing on the Image of God within us allows us to respond to conventional theological questions in another way. Does God hear our prayers? Does God answer our prayers? Does God act in history? Does God care? Belief in the divine Image within internalizes and reverses these questions. The questions now turn reflexive. Do I hear? Do I respond? Do I intervene? Do I care? Our questions about God are God's questions about us. Where the immanent Image is denied or ignored, the dialogue between divinity and humanity is broken off. As the late-nineteenth-century rabbi Elijah Benamozegh asserted, "When we seek God, it is God who seeks Himself in us" (*Israel and Humanity,* 1995).

The Image within binds heaven and earth. The whispered voice of the internal Image is not in the heavens above nor in the oceans beneath. It is close to you, in your mouth and in your heart that you may act on it (Deuteronomy 30:14). The passage to the eternal is internal.

Self-Awareness and the Significance of the Rites

To recover the sanctity of the rites of passage we need to become aware of the revolutionary implications that follow from the belief in the endowed Image of God. What we celebrate in every stage of life is the divine potentiality inherent in us. In the first century C.E., Rabbi Akiva said, "Beloved is man, for he was created in the Image of God. But it was by a special love that it was made known to him that he was created in the Image of God" (Talmud, *Taanit* 11a, 11b). Self-awareness of the Image is central to the spiritual renaissance of the ritual life.

Despite the wretched record of humans' ability to deface the Image, despite the personal failures and tragedies of the self, the tradition clings to the possibilities, potentialities, and purposes of the Image. No notion of inherited sin can destroy the sacred character of the Image. A contemporary Orthodox thinker, J. B. Soloveitchik, refers to the "innermost core of the soul that remains something pure, precious and sacred in man's soul" (*On Repentance,* 1980). To acknowledge the Image within us is to affirm belief in the possibility of repentance, transformation, and renewal of the self. Consciousness of the divine Image within brings to the foreground awareness of what we may become and what the world may become. Soloveitchik asserts of the human being, "No one can help him. He is his own redeemer; he is his own messiah who has come to redeem him from the darkness of his exile to the light of his personal redemption" (ibid.). In the process of self-transformation, the human being assumes the role of co-creator. As interpreted in the tradition, God implanted in us an ideal Image with the capacity to renew ourselves and ascend to a higher level. The Image is the companion at every station of our development, a presence in every rite of passage.

A Legend of Hiddenness

To help recover the ritual life that sanctifies our existence, the dignity and power of the Image of God within us must be recovered. A legend of its hiddenness tells of a group of angels who, having heard that God intended to create the human being in God's own likeness, plotted to hide the Image. One angel proposed hiding it on the pinnacle of the highest mountain. But a wiser angel pointed out that the human is an ambitious climber and would ascend the highest mountain. Another angel suggested that the Image be sunk beneath the deepest ocean. But this angel too was dissuaded from the plan when it was pointed out that the human is curious and would plumb the ocean and draw forth the hidden treasure. The shrewdest angel counseled that the Image should be hidden within the human beings themselves because it is the last place that they would be likely to look. For us, that must be the first place to look.

✦ *The Image*

What ties them together
    the rites of passage
      that mark life's journey?
What thread traces the three tenses of our path?

An Image implanted in each soul's being
Fashioned with the breath of Love.
This Image, not identical with the Imageless Creator,
But a divine impression
Upon a soul yearning to be realized.

The Image, not born complete
But gifted with limitless potentiality
Capacities to grow and to change
To heal and transform.

The Image, endangered
By debris of conceit and greed
Buried beneath the dust of petty ambition.

Prayers and study
Seek to free the Image
From the clutter of smallness
Distracting from the largesse
Of its dreams.

The Image, with us morning, noon, and night,
In birth, holding out the promises of possibilities
In the bar/bat mitzvah, celebrating the developing moral conscience
In sickness, encouraging curative powers
In marriage, joining one Image to another
In death, surviving the body through its legacy to progeny.
A gift to be earned
A seed to be nourished
A tree of life to be cultivated
A promise to be kept.

As this infant has entered the covenant so may this child enter the world of *Torah, chupah,* and *maasim tovim*—moral wisdom, marital bliss, and the practice of good deeds.

Rabbi's Manual

1

ell

BIRTH AND *B'RIT*
Covenanting the Child in God's Image

Ritual, like poetry, art, and philosophy in an overwhelmingly pragmatic and utilitarian society, has a difficult time justifying its practice. If any rationale for ritual practice is credible, it tends toward the hygienic. Kosher is for the sake of cleanliness, the Sabbath for alleviating the stress of the weekday, fasting on Yom Kippur is a purgative, a cleansing of the system, and circumcision is justified as a prevention of cancer. A doctor friend expresses amazement at the prescience of the ancient Jews who knew that the appropriate time to have the child circumcised was on the eighth day because "then the child has a sufficient amount of vitamin K, which is indispensable for the blood-clotting mechanism." Such medical rationalization of ritual not only distorts its history, but ignores the spiritual meaning threaded throughout ritual symbolism.

A child is born, a new life has been created, we have given birth to a being with incalculable ritual potentialities for whose actualization we are prepared to assume profound responsibility. The poetry and philosophy raise the phenomenon of birth from the purely biological into a spiritual realm. Birth is a miraculous event. That miracle need not be understood as a supernatural intervention that violates the laws of nature but as a natural event that promises the power to transform lives. The twelfth-century Jewish philosopher and physician Moses Maimonides noted the odd piety that is blind to the miracles within the horizons of the natural. He observed, with no little irony, that were we to explain to some pious sages that it is God who sends a fiery angel to enter the womb of a woman and to form a fetus there, it would be accepted as a religious account of God's miraculous power and wisdom. But oddly, they would be repelled by the explanation that God "has placed in the sperm a formative force shaping the limbs and giving them their configuration" (*Guide to the Perplexed,* pt. 2, chapt. 6). To have a child is a miracle in the sense that its Hebrew translation captures. The word for "miracle" in Hebrew is *neis,* literally "a sign," an event of SIGN-nificance, an event that signifies something of superordinate importance in our lives. In the Septuagint, the Greek translation of the Bible, the Hebrew term *neis* is appropriately translated as *semeion,* "a sign." In the biblical sense of *neis,* the birth and *b'rit*-covenant of the infant signals a natural event of transforming significance. The child inducted into a covenantal community of faith profoundly alters the life of the immediate family and its community.

Why We Rise

When on the eighth day after the birth the infant is brought into the room to be covenanted and named, all the assembled are bidden to rise. Family and friends, young and old, cry out, "*Baruch haba:* Blessed be He who comes to enter the covenant." Before whom do they stand? Whom do they greet? We read in the midrash: "When a human being goes on the road, a troop of angels proceeds before him and proclaims: 'Make way for the Image of God'" (*D'varim Rabbah, R'eih* 4:4). Those assembled rise and bless this infant, who enters the world with a pure soul, untainted by any inherited sin, unblemished by any transgression. No Jewish ceremony is needed to absolve the infant's sins, no exorcism is called upon to purge the demons. The infant is born innocent. We rise before a child touched by the finger of God, who contains within the potential powers of the divine Image to help mend the world.

Why the Baby Cries

Why then, the Rabbis mused, do babies enter life in tears? A rabbinic legend attempting to account for the crying of the infant when it emerges from the womb reveals profound insights into the Jewish view of human nature and its purposes. In an imaginative rabbinic midrash, the baby is said to cry because it is reluctant to leave the realm of pure souls to enter a world of impurity. So the legend explains, when a woman conceives, the Angel of Night carries the sperm before God, who then decrees what manner of human being it shall become. Will it be male or female, strong or weak, rich or poor, beautiful or ugly, fat or thin? But, significantly, no decree is announced as to whether it will be good or evil. That determination is left to the human being, for it is that which expresses the unique human capacity to choose. God will not coerce the human being to be good or to believe, because the essential dignity of the human being is in the free choice to act and to believe. The legend continues the tale with God signaling an angel to bring forth a soul that is hidden away among others in Paradise. God issues a command to the soul: "Enter the sperm." The soul cries: "Lord of the universe, I am well pleased with Paradise, in which I have been living. Why do you dismiss me to enter this impure sperm, I who am holy and pure and a part of Your glory?" God responds: "Do not cry. The world that I caused you to enter is better than the world from which you come. I created you only for the purpose of entering this world."

We are left to consider in what sense this world is better than Paradise. It brings to mind a comment of Rabbi Jacob, who in *Pirkei Avot* asserts that "one hour in this world of repentance and good deeds is better than the whole life of the world to come" (*Pirkei Avot* 4:21). It is not in Paradise, not in the place enjoyed by the soul before life is created, nor in the place enjoyed after the death of the righteous, that the human being is free to exercise the potentiality to live out the attributes of godliness. It is here in this world that the human being can mend the torn fabric of the world. In that sense, the world that the soul now enters is better than the world from which it came.

The Cleft on the Upper Lip

A related legend wonders about the indentation on the upper lip of the newly arrived infant. How did this anatomical oddity come about? It is told that before birth, an angel leads the soul around heaven and hell and shows it where it will live on earth and where it will die and be buried.

Yet before the babe emerges from the womb, an angel taps it above the upper lip, which forces a cleft on the upper lip, causing the light of the world to be extinguished. Now the soul forgets everything that it had been shown and learned. What is the meaning of this symbolic amnesia? It suggests that while there is innate knowledge in the human being, it can be brought forth only through human effort. Wisdom is realized through the experience of living, not through the passive reception of a gift before birth. Moral knowledge is gained not through inheritance, but by active search. The discoveries must be gained by human effort. Not in heaven but on earth is the struggle to know enacted. On earth the real and the ideal meet, and through their transaction, the Image is further realized.

Why the Covenant

On the eighth day the infant reenters this world and gains a new status through the covenant. He or she becomes a co-creator with God, a partner with God responsible to help transform the uncompleted world. We note here a significant aspect of the reality principle of Judaism: the world is created incomplete. Everything in the world calls for improvement. When asked why, if God so loved circumcision, God did not create every male child circumcised, the Sages point to the imperfection of the entire world, including people. To be a covenanted partner with God is to help perfect it. "The mustard seed must be sweetened, the lupine must be softened, the wheat must be ground, and the human being must be perfected" (*Tanchuma, B'reishit* 7f, 10a). The divine Image is no exception, for it is not born complete. It needs to be cultivated, refined, perfected. Alongside the Jewish reality principle of the imperfection of the world stands the Jewish ideality principle that assigns to the human being the task of turning the world that "is" into the world that "ought to be." The world created, while not perfect, is perfectible. We are not born holy, but we can sanctify the ways of our life.

This spiritual mandate explains why the *b'rit,* or covenant, takes place on the eighth day even if the eighth day is the Sabbath or coincides with Yom Kippur. For after seven days, the infant has lived through the act of the creation of this world in which the child is to participate. On the eighth day, this covenanted child is more than a passive part of nature, but rather a human agent actively engaged in the development of a moral universe. The guardians of this baby are mandated to nurture this sacred life so that this potentiality may be actualized.

Why the Minyan

In the Middle Ages, a custom arose that twelve candles were lit at the *b'rit,* signifying the twelve tribes of Israel into which the infant is inducted. The child is enveloped in the embrace of community. While the *b'rit* was traditionally a celebration involving the male infant, increasingly today covenant ceremonies are created for daughters. Parents are encouraged to further personalize the covenant by writing their own dreams for their child, their commitments to provide a family environment that will nourish the child's growth. (That statement of aspiration at the day of the covenant may be read thirteen years later on the day of the child's bar/bat mitzvah.) The infant is given a name and the traditional benediction is recited: "As the child has entered the covenant, so may he/she enter the world of Torah, marriage, and the practice of good deeds." The benediction contains the threefold goals of the human being in its spiritual journey. Whatever the chosen vocation or profession may be, a person's spiritual career should include the quest for moral wisdom, consecrated love, and the practice of justice and mercy.

Traditionally, the father is bound to see to it that his male child is circumcised. If there is no father present or if the child should have a father who does not see to it that he is circumcised, the obligation falls upon the *beit din,* the representatives of the Jewish community. If the child should be an orphan and have no father, a moving prayer is recited: "Thou God of all flesh, father of orphans, be Thou a father unto him and he will be a son unto Thee. May his entering into the covenant be a comfort and a solace to his mother and all his family." That compassionate prayer reminds us that the community plays a responsible role in the rites of passage. The minyan, ten Jews above the age of thirteen, is the minimum required for congregational worship and public Torah reading. In Jewish thought, holiness involves community. This precept is derived from the verse in Leviticus (22:32) in which God declares, "I will be sanctified among the Children of Israel." God is sanctified not in a holy place but in a living community. Communion with God is found through community. There are, of course, acts of holiness in solitariness. But we cannot as easily come to God, leaping vertically out of the skin of our insular individuality. We come to God, as it were, horizontally. In the absence of a father, the community assumes responsibility for fulfilling the covenant. "Even if my father and mother abandon me, the Lord will take me in" (Psalm 27:10). The community, in God's stead, takes on that role. The interdependence of self and community is further evidenced in the Talmud: "If a community is in trouble, let no one say, 'I will go to my house, eat and drink, and declare peace with you my soul'" (*Taanit* 11a).

The birth of a child summons the family together. The parents assign the child a name, which includes the name of the father and mother. The severed umbilical cord does not detach the child from the family, and at the *b'rit* the family acknowledges its mutual attachment to the child and to the community. The boundary of the self does not end at the periphery of the body. The members of the family who surround the infant recall their dependence, their need for the mutual comfort, protection, and wisdom of *mishpachah*. Through the ritual covenant of the child, the members of the family are re-covenanted.

Pidyon HaBen/Pidyon HaBat:
Dedication of the Child on the Thirty-First Day

Traditionally, on the thirty-first day after his birth, the firstborn male of the mother is redeemed from priestly service (Exodus 13:13). At the *pidyon* ceremony, the father pays a sum of five shekels or its equivalent to a *Kohein,* or Jewish priest.

The origin and rationale for this ritual are obscure. Some scholars believe that this redemption ceremony is a thanksgiving offering for God's sparing the firstborn Hebrew sons from the tenth plague that slew the firstborn of the Egyptians.

Others suggest that the redemption of the firstborn ceremony reflects the biblical struggle against the heathen practice of human sacrifice, particularly the sacrifice of the firstborn child. Evidence of child sacrifice is scattered throughout the Bible. We read of two Jewish kings, Achaz and Menasseh, who consigned their sons to fire (II Kings 16:3, 21:6).

Inveighing against such cultic practices, the prophet Micah asks ironically, "With what should I approach the Lord, do homage to God on high? Shall I approach Him with burnt offerings, with calves of a year old? . . . Shall I give my firstborn for my transgression, the first fruit of my sins?" (Micah 6:6–7). Micah is repulsed by the perversion of the central meaning of worship and sums up the essence of true piety: "He hath told you, O man, what is good and what the Lord requires of you. Only to do justice and to love goodness and to walk modestly with your God" (Micah 6:8).

The revolutionary break with the human sacrifice of paganism is enacted in the biblical story of the binding of Isaac. Abraham hears the voice of God commanding him to take "thy son, thine only son, whom you love, even Isaac and get you into the land of Moriah, and offer him there for a burnt offering upon one of the mountains that I will tell you" (Genesis 22:2). The denouement of this exchange concludes with a complete reversal of God's command. The angel of God countermands the initial imperative of God. The angel of God cries out, "Do not raise your hand against the boy, or do anything to him" (Genesis 22:12).

Seen in this light, the *pidyon* ceremony reinforces the lesson learned from the biblical account of the binding of Isaac. The child, whose viability we celebrate, is created as an end in himself and is not to be used as a means, even to demonstrate our loyalty to God. We do not come closer to God by binding Isaac to the altar, but by releasing him to a life of freedom.

The child is redeemed from bondage to idolatry and superstition. The *pidyon* is not a redemption of the child from service to God, but a dedication to the service of God.

There are increasing numbers of Jews who do not restrict the *pidyon* ceremony to males only, but include their month-old daughters as well. The Image of God bears no gender, "male and female created God them" (Genesis 1:27). At the dedication of the daughter, the five shekels are contributed to a cause that the family chooses in honor of their newborn child. Favorite passages from Psalms and Proverbs are recited. "Blessed are You, Creator of the universe, who has kept us in life, sustained us, and enabled us to reach this day of sanctity."

Meditations

✦ *From Where Did You Come?*

From where did you arrive?
Out of the womb of Eve and the seed of Adam.
Angels showed your unborn soul
The secrets of heaven and earth.
Your soul pleaded with God not to push you
From the comfort of the womb.

And God answered:
Do not cry,
Do not be afraid,
The world you enter is the better world
You have lived in innocence.

Here, you will be My ally, My witness,
My co-creator, My co-sanctifier.
Here is your place,
Here, confirm My name,
Here, bring strength to those who inhabit the world,
Here, offer testimony of My goodness.
Welcome to this world.

✦ *Cleft on the Upper Lip*

The infant comes into this world with former wisdom.
At birth, an angel strikes the baby
on the upper lip, leaves an indented mark.
With that blow, the child forgets all it has learned
in another world.

That forgetfulness is a blessing.
Not the answer
But the quest for truth is the goal of life.
It is not the given from another world
But the struggle in this world that brings wisdom.
Buried in us, a wisdom dwells in our inner soul
for us to bring forth.

May this child be blessed
With the courage to recover
The wisdom to achieve consecrated love
With heart, mind, and spine for the practice of good deeds.

The infant is brought into the room.
All rise, old and young, family and friends.
A newborn has entered our world,
We stand in its honor.
This infant comes innocent, pure of body and pure of soul.
No stain on its soul, no blemish on its spirit.
This infant comes from a world of benediction
into a world awaiting his benediction.

"Whenever you see the footprints of human beings,
God stands before you.
Whenever human beings walk abroad, a company of angels
precedes and calls out, 'Make way for the image of God.' "

(D'varim Rabbah 4:4)

✦ *On the Eighth Day*

Even on the Sabbath,
Even during Festival or fast,
The *b'rit* takes place on the eighth day.
Sabbath or *Yom Tov* or Yom Kippur,
A reminder of the constancy
Entwining our life with God's, the covenant.

On the eighth day our child is covenanted,
Having lived through the Sabbath,
No stranger to Creation,
No passive particle,
Thrown into the world.
Our child is partner,
Co-worker, *shutaf,* co-creator, co-sanctifier
Of the Source of all being.

May our child grow with purpose.
Ameliorate pain,
Straighten the bent,
Raise the fallen,
Protect the innocent,
Loosen the chains of the bound.

Through this infant,
covenanted to a life of transformation,
We give thanks for the renewal of Creation
Every day, every hour, every moment.

✦ *Parents: Reflections at Birth*

We are not born enough.
When we were first born
We were not aware.

God has given us another birth,
Flesh of our flesh, blood of our blood,
Drawn from the marrow of our bones.

Before us lies a mystery of possibilities.
Who knows what dreams
Lie dormant in this tiny body soul?

This much we know:
This infant
Upon whom we smile, offers wordless joys,
Opens dreams of tomorrow's tomorrow.
Tomorrow has a different significance today.

We rise
To greet the child with blessing, *Baruch haba b'shem Adonai,*
Blessed are you who comes in the name of the Lord,
Blessed be You who brings us the promise of blessing.

✦ *Whose Am I?*

Not "Who am I?"
But "Whose am I?"
In belonging lies the secret.

Who belongs to me?
To whom do I belong?
Who accepts me?
Whom do I accept?
Who has claims upon me?
Upon whom do I lay claim?

Who knows my failings?
Who knows the meanings
Of my angers and ambitions, my fears,
My cries for love sometimes hidden past recognition?

Whose am I?
The umbilical cord must be torn,
Incestuous ties severed.
Yet untied, I seek renewed connection
Beyond the womb.

Who am I?
Whose am I?
My name, my people, my God.

✦ *In My Arms*

In my arms a child is held
    a nameless being
       possessed of unknown potentialities.
In my arms an infant is held
Upon whom we confer in the presence of his/her people
A name to be known in Israel as _____ ben/bat
                                  Child's Hebrew Name

_____.

                Parents' Hebrew Names

That name includes our own.
In parenting this child,
We are forever bound to each other.

In our arms a child is cradled
    no stranger thrown into an alien world,
    but a human being born into a faith, culture, tradition.
This child belongs to our people.
Upon us, this child has claims.
Upon this child, the community has claims.

In our arms, a child is embraced
    a child of God,
    into whose nostrils the wind of life was breathed
    by the spirit of godliness.

This name is a dream, a hope, an oath
    for *Torah*—moral wisdom
    for *chupah*—sanctified love
    for *maasim tovim*—the practice of good deeds.

May the name be a blessing
    to his/her family, his/her people, and humankind
    and to God in whose image this child was created.

✦ *Touch My Heart*

Child
Touch my nose, my lips, my eyes
    with your small hands.
Touch my arms and chest.
Feel their shape
    how real they are.

Now, touch my love.
No, not my chest or arms or lips.
You are puzzled.
How is one to touch love
    and where is its place?

Love is not here or there
But who would
    deny its reality?
Where does love reside
    if it cannot be pointed to?
Is it less than my chin?
If anything, love is sharper, harder, softer,
    warmer than what I can touch.

There are matters not subject to the senses
    taste, sound, smell, sight, touch
Love elusive to definition
    yet known without doubt.
Known to make us cry and laugh
    to move us to unimagined heights
    to courage and self-sacrifice.
    Experiences—like love or God
    Cannot be fingered, placed, or poked.
    Of such things
Not where but when.

Not where is love
Not where is God
    But when is love
    When is God.
Recall the meeting
    the moment, the time.

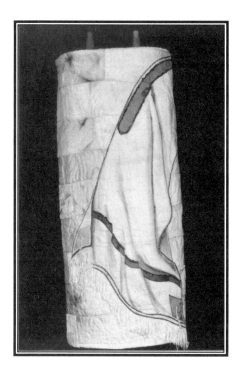

Protect my children from my secret wish to make them over in my image and illusion. Let them move to the music that they love dissonant perhaps to me.

Ezekiel Nissim

2

BAR/BAT MITZVAH
Re-parenting

Franz Kafka, in his letter to his father cited in the introduction, recalled his bar mitzvah as "some ridiculous learning by heart . . . that led to nothing but something like the ridiculous passing of an examination." His is a familiar complaint. But more is at stake than the mouthing of a tape recording of the biblical and prophetic passages. Such mimicry is pedagogically corrigible by the institutions of learning. There are, however, basic moral issues that threaten to ridicule the passage from childhood to adulthood that involve the family.

A number of rabbinic statements suggest that at the end of the thirteenth year the conscience of the child emerges. The bar and bat mitzvah are referred to as *b'nei deiah,* persons of reason, or *b'nei onshin,* persons accountable for interpersonal transactions, and are counted in the minyan of ten Jews required for worship services. How is that birth of conscience experienced within the family in the preparation of the *simchah?*

Peer Pressure

Planning for the bar/bat mitzvah is an affair of the family. Decisions as to the character of the celebration present another opportunity for the members of the family to find each other in Judaism.

There are ethical issues involved in the decision that reveal the values of the family and shape the character of the celebrant. One of the repeated concerns in planning the reception deals with the limits of the entertainment. The adolescent celebrant often feels peer pressure to keep up with his or her friends, especially in the realm of the celebratory extravaganza. The child may have attended the receptions of others in which few restraints have been imposed on their size or expense. The child confronts the parents with the irresistible mantra: "Everybody does it." The family needs to come together to decide how to respond to this persistent argument. Parents must themselves be convinced that the argument "everyone does it" is not a moral way of thinking and then teach this to their children. Essential to the bar/bat mitzvah passage whose rites we celebrate is the children's awareness of what is right and wrong and the moral implications of their decisions. The b'nei mitzvah, celebrating their moral coming of age, need to hear a principled counteraction to the "everyone does it" incantation. Parents can explain that the rationalization "everyone does it" can be used to justify almost anything others may do, whatever its merit: cheating on exams, taking drugs, sexual exploitation, and violence. "Everyone does it" is a mind-set readily turned to rationalize bribery, income tax evasion, and infidelity. Parents may in good conscience explain: "We are not everyone. We are not lemmings following everyone into the sea." The decisions a family makes about the bar/bat mitzvah celebration is a reflection of the ethical values of the family.

Some parents report that their children murmur that the modest reception the parents propose is "cheap" and contrary to their social stature. The children may be told that the issue is not a matter of their ability to afford the expense. There may be money enough for the most exorbitant extravaganza. But in accordance with Jewish values, *hasin al mamonum shel Yisrael,* one must be sparing and morally wise with the use of money. As for the child's accusations of parental parsimony, they can point out that restraint is not cheap. Conspicuous consumption is cheap, showing off is tawdry, wastefulness is vulgar, exhibition of narcissism is petty. What is elegant and magnanimous is to use the money to purchase blankets for those who shiver in the cold, to tithe gifts for Mazon in response to world hunger, to provide scholarships for those who cannot afford the blessings of education. Elegant is to have table centerpieces of books for libraries and cans of food for those who are in need. The family must make it clear that the bar/bat mitzvah celebrates the mature, ethical idealism of Judaism in their lives and that *tzedakah* calls for personal tithing for the sake of the needs of others. Relative to this discussion, one family was reminded of the scene in *Schindler's List* in which Oscar Schindler, surrounded by hundreds of Jews he had saved, gazes at his car and cries, "The car, the car. Why did I keep the car? It would have bought ten more lives."

Becoming bar/bar mitzvah is an opportunity for the moral sensibility in the child to be tapped, valued, and encouraged. Family conversations at this stage of the child's development are significant. Parents create memories, and memories create character. The memory we would have our children recall is not of the menu, the flowers, the costly games, but the embracing sense of moral purpose that connects the earlier ceremony at the sanctuary with the celebration in the social hall. Those are the memories that solidify and elevate the family.

The Ethics of Family Inclusion

The bar/bat mitzvah is the featured celebrant. But the bar/bat mitzvah event is a family affair in which definitions and boundaries are drawn. The decision as to who will receive the invitation contains a moral agenda of its own. The invitation appears as the local equivalent to the Israeli "Law of Return," determining who is entitled to unquestioned entry to the Promised Land of our ancestry. The invitation to the bar/bat mitzvah indicates whom we welcome as members of the *mishpachah* and whom we exclude. Do we, for example, invite Aunt Rose, who was married to Uncle Abe and who, since his death, has been distanced from the family? Who is to receive which honors at the ceremony, and who is to be seated with whom? Shall we invite the teacher of the bat mitzvah? What does it mean to the teacher to be so remembered, and what does it mean to the child to remember the teacher? The bar/bat mitzvah passage often includes a rediscovery of the *mishpachah*. It entails decisions that bring awareness of the scope and character of our family identity.

In Whose Image?

The Talmud speaks of the child being raised by three partners: the father, the mother, and God (Talmud, *Kiddushin* 30b). All three are to be honored.

The parents should realize the pedagogic implications of the belief that the child is created in God's Image. To be created in God's Image means that the child should not be treated as a clone of parental ambitions. For parents to respect the Image of God in the child is to overcome the natural parental narcissistic impulse to see the child as a chip off the old block. Parents respectful of the Image of God in the child will guard against the societal pressures that view the child as a "*naches*-producing machine," measured solely in terms of the extrinsic marks of institutional academic success or popularity. Understanding the Image within the child means recognition of the entire child. The parent is to take account of the spiritual intelligence of the child, recognizing and nurturing qualities such as kindness and compassion, virtues less frequently praised in our competitive society. Idolatry is the worship of a part as if it were the whole. The narrow meritocracy that has enveloped us mimics a form of idolatry that regards a part of the child as if it were the whole child. This mismeasurement distorts the Image that is expressed in the goodness, empathic intelligence, resilience, and optimism of the child.

The Image is the theological ground of human self-esteem. It insists that the child is not his I.Q. or SAT score. And it is also, not incidentally, a reminder to the parents that they too are not simply the sum total of their material accomplishments and acquisitions. As parents regard their children, they come to regard themselves. The bar/bat mitzvah can mark a maturing transformation of the members of the family.

A Second Parenting

The bar/bat mitzvah passage provides an opportune occasion to reexamine the relationships between the parent and the adolescent. Parents are, at times, gods to their children. But a careful study of the Bible instructs us that even God as parent is subject to frustration and failure. At the end of the Creation story of Genesis, God is portrayed as disillusioned with the sons and daughters whom God had made in the divine Image. "The Lord saw how great was man's wickedness on earth. . . . And the Lord regretted that He had made man on earth, and His heart was saddened. The Lord said, 'I will blot out from the earth the men whom I have created . . . for I regret that I made them' " (Genesis 6:5–7). The behavior of these children was not as God had expected. The Image with which the human being is invested is an aspiration, not a completed realization.

God recognizes God's failure. God had overidealized these children, expected too much from them. God faces reality and learns the limits of the divine children who are "evil from youth" (Genesis 8:21). God had originally thought that these children would not be so violent, so hungry for the blood and flesh of animals, unable to eat off the herbs yielding seed and the fruit of the trees that God had freely promised them.

What is to be done with such disillusionment? God re-parents. God proposes a new covenant different from the first. God alters the standards to accommodate to the limitations of God's children. In the second covenant God declares, "Every moving thing that lives shall be for food for you, as the green herb have I given you all" (Genesis 9:3). God no longer demands the unrealistic ideals God had had for these children in the Garden of Eden. After the Flood, God compromises and enters into a second covenant with humanity. "Only flesh with the life thereof, which is the blood thereof, shall you not eat" (Genesis 9:4). Only one refrain from the first covenant remains intact: "For in the Image of God made He man" (Genesis 9:6).

If God can err, human parents can also acknowledge their errancy. To recognize a mistake is not the end of the world. God can re-covenant, and parents can re-parent. The time of the bar/bat mitzvah can be a perfect opportunity to enter into a new covenant of understanding with all the members of the family. The child as well as the parent may be freed of the drivenness and compulsiveness of achievement that is self-imposed upon all the members of the family. Parents and children can be freed of the loveless meritocracy by appreciating the Image with which they were each created. The family can discover the core of its own continuity, unity, and idealism in the course of celebrating the sacred moments in the life of its young. What unites the family is not the resemblance of the DNA components of the members, but the shared tradition of moral culture that is passed on intergenerationally through the symbols and sentiments marking the transitions of life.

The rites of passage are family events in which the theology of the synagogue and its community are personalized at home. Celebrations do not begin or end in the synagogue. They begin in the sanctuary of the home, around the altar of the family table, and continue in the renewed relationships among the members of *mishpachah.* Wherever the family meets for its formal celebration, it passes the mezuzah of the home, the text that is affixed to the threshold between home and world and includes these instructions: "Impress them upon your children. Recite them when you stay at home and when you are away, when you lie down and when you rise up" (Deuteronomy 6:7).

Meditations

✦ *A Parent's Perspective*

You are not today as you were yesterday,
Nor are we.
Something has occurred.

We sit with the congregation,
You stand alone on the *bimah.*
You lead the congregation,
We follow.
You sing, pray, speak,
We listen.

Not a mere echo of our sound,
You have words of your own.
The still, small voice of conscience stands alone
Stronger in you now than ever before.
A blessed distance between us,
You are ours but also your own.

You were called to the Torah,
Your name and our names interwoven,
You are not us,
We are not you,
But we are inseparable.

✦ *The Day After*

It is over now
    The chanting, the speech,
    The candies, the gifts,
    The band, the music,
It is the next day, the day beyond.

Now the real choice begins.
Now you are responsible, accountable,
It is you who must choose.

Will you choose to live what you have spoken?
Or will those promises, rapturous sentiments
Waft aimlessly in the air, clinging to the ceiling of the synagogue?

The ceremony is over
    Will you shut the Book,
    Shelve the texts,
    Prematurely end your growth?

Or will you continue to flourish
    In fidelity to our people,
    In mastery of our culture?

Will you take your place
    Beside those who have sanctified the world,
    Bring them the vitality of your youth,
    Share with them the freshness of your promise?

It is over now.
You no longer face the congregation.
It is the day after and you stand alone
Before the mirror of your soul.

✦ *A Parent's Ambition*

"Protect my children from my secret wish
    to make them over in my image and illusions.
Let them move to the music that they love
    dissonant perhaps to me." (Ezekiel Nissim)

We have raised them, sculpted them, schooled them,
Exposed them to our ways and our world.
Who can blame our parental conceit,
Imposing our dreams on their heads.

Give us the courage and wisdom
To sever the incestuous ties
Free them from the bondage of mimicry.
Not in our image are they created,
Extensions of our ambitions,
Duplications of our aspirations.

Let them imitate God, not us.
Let them be freed of servitude to anyone.
Give us the wisdom to let go of them,
The moral way to hold them close.

✦ *My Grandson's Bar Mitzvah*

My grandson, a bar mitzvah.
Child of my child called to the Torah.
Bringing one face to face with the future.
Geography has distanced us.
I have not raised him,
Nor given him instruction,
Bound his wounds, absorbed his sobs,
Rallied him to victory.

Yet from the distance
I have heard and imagined
His defeats and triumphs.

Now here he is
For me to see.
I listen to a chant, a prayer, a benediction
I too once sang.

Now
Before family and friends,
I receive unmerited blessing.

In him,
I am continued.
In his chanting
Is confirmation of my immortality.

A grandson in the presence of our community,
Alone, on his own two feet.
We are bound together as never before,
My grandson and I.

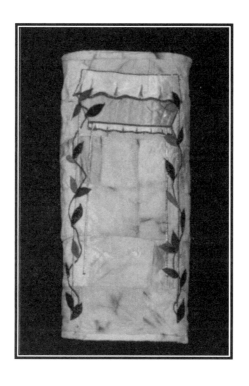

Praised are You, Lord our God, Ruler of the universe who created joy and gladness, bride and groom, mirth, song, delight and rejoicing, love and harmony, peace and companionship. May these be heard in the cities of Judah and in the streets of Jerusalem, voices of joy and gladness, voices of those joined in marriage under the bridal canopy, the voice of young people, feasting and singing. Praised are You, Lord, who causes the groom and bride to rejoice.

The Seventh Benediction of the Wedding Ceremony

3

THE WEDDING

I and Thou

Twoness

The verse from Genesis reads: "In the image of God created He him; male and female created He them" (Genesis 1:27). "Him"—singular, "them"—plural. This curious locution in this first version of Creation gave rise to the legend that Adam was originally created a hermaphrodite, an androgynous human being possessed of male and female characteristics. The mythic primordial Adam, though sexually self-sufficient, bemoaned his loneliness. Out of compassion, God split Adam in half, "made of him two backs, one back on this side and one back on the other side" (*B'reishit Rabbah* 8:1). Now Adam was divided into separate male and female genders, each yearning for a reunion with the other, each looking for its better half. In marriage, one Image of God reaches out to enter into relationship with another Image of God. It is not good for the Image to dwell alone. "It is not good that the man should be alone; I will make a fitting helper for him" (Genesis 2:18). "Therefore shall a man leave his father and his mother and shall cleave unto his wife, and they shall be one flesh" (Genesis 2:24). The ideal is to become as one, close but not identical, one but not the same.

Before separation, Adam was an undifferentiated self. After separation, a profound human desire emerges: to reunite with the "better half" while preserving the unique self. Before the separation, distance was missing. The other was absorbed in the self, swallowed without recognition of the uniqueness of the other. The new union in marriage respects the sameness and difference of the "I" and "thou." This other, like myself, is created in God's Image and is not to be made over in my own likeness. The other is not an ear into which I may shout my ambition and frustration. The other is a "thou" to be heard. The dialogue must not be turned into a soliloquy. I cannot say "thou" to myself. Marriage calls for a wisdom of love, the art to achieve the delicate balance between singularity and unity. The myth of the creation of primordial man and primordial woman out of an individual self teaches the subtle arithmetic of love: one becomes two, and two become one.

The "I" is better understood in relationship than in aloneness. I know myself better when I am with another. In the face-to-face encounter with the other, the "I" of each partner is revealed. The critical preposition of the "I" is "with." How am I with the other's joy and with the other's sadness? How am I with the other's health and with the other's illness? How am I with the other's triumph and with the other's failure?

The Image of God is burnished through relationship. In relationship, responsibility, compassion, feeling, and respect are exhibited and verified. Godliness is experienced through attachment with an other. Martin Buber accounts for this connection when he asks, "Would you believe? Then love."

Jewish mystics characteristically play with the numerical equivalent of the Hebrew alphabet to reveal its deeper truths, known as *g'matria.* The Hebrew word for "love," *ahavah,* numerically adds up to thirteen. Twice thirteen is twenty-six, which is numerically equivalent to the term *Adonai,* "God." When two honor the Image of the Divine within each other, there God resides.

At the wedding ceremony, the bride and groom are blessed with seven benedictions, symbolizing the original seven days of Creation that are renewed each day. One of the seven benedictions reads: "Blessed are You, Lord, our God, Ruler of all the world, who has made the human being in Your Image, after Your likeness, and hast prepared out of Your very self a perpetual fabric of life. Blessed are You, O Lord, Creator of the human being." The wedding reflects a personal and cosmic event, a union of heaven and earth. The world was not created only once. The daily prayer book refers to God as renewing the world in goodness every day. When two separate beings are drawn together and committed to renew the world, the world is re-created. The whole world, a Chasidic master declared, was created for the sake of union.

The Chupah—*The Wedding Canopy*

The place of the ceremony is beneath the *chupah,* the wedding canopy. The *chupah* represents the home and is not cloistered but is open on all four sides. The home that the bride and groom will establish is not shut off from the world but open to it. Fixed on the doorpost of the home is a welcoming signature, the mezuzah, a sealed box that contains a small roll of parchment on which is written the biblical verse the *Sh'ma,* declaring the unity of God and God's creation. Additionally, it contains two biblical passages concerning the love of God (Deuteronomy 6:4–9; 11:13–21). Included in those verses is the instruction to teach your children "when you lie down and when you rise up." Based on that verse, two conflicting opinions arose as to the proper placement of the mezuzah on the doorpost. Since it is written "when you rise up," the eleventh-century biblical commentator Rashi concluded that the mezuzah should be attached to the doorpost vertically. His grandson Rabbenu Tam, however, stressed that the passage reading "when you lie down" suggests that the mezuzah should be placed horizontally. An important compromise was effected: the mezuzah is affixed in a slanting position. This position is symbolically instructive. The true strength of love lies not in rigidity, my way or no way, but in compromise, concession, and compassion born of mutual respect.

The mezuzah is placed on the doorpost of the threshold of the home to remind the members of the family to carry the sacred values of the home into the world without. A Chasidic interpretation adds that a beggar whose eyes are lowered out of embarrassment, because he comes to solicit, raises his eyes toward the mezuzah and is reminded of his true worth as a child of God.

Wedding Wine

Wine is drunk by the bride and groom several times during the wedding ceremony. Wine has a history redolent with theological meaning. Among the pagans, it was associated with Dionysus, the god of wine, and with bacchanalian drunken revelry. To counter this excess, some religious traditions condemned wine as the devil's potion and prohibited its consumption. Judaism took a different stance toward wine. It was sublimated. Neither demonized nor sacralized, wine was understood as an ambiguous energy to be sanctified for noble use. Wine is used for *Kiddush,* the prayer and ceremony by which the holiness of the Sabbath and Festivals is proclaimed. "Wine cheers the heart of man," Psalm 104 declares. It is good to rejoice with the bridegroom and bride, and so one of the seven benedictions under the wedding *chupah* praises God, "who created joy and gladness, bride and groom, mirth, song, delight and rejoicing, love and harmony, peace and companionship." In itself, wine is neither sacred nor profane. Wine, like other substances and energies in life, is an ambivalent energy. Wine can lift up the spirit or sink it into drunken stupor. So too with love. Love can liberate the soul of another or suffocate it through absorption. Everything depends upon the purpose to which we use God's gifts.

The *Kiddush* blessing over wine, "who creates the fruit of the vine," could have been recited over grapes. But wine, not grapes, is used for the *Kiddush* sanctification because wine is a product of human energy and intelligence in cooperation with the givenness of nature. Therein lies the special character of the *Kiddush* sanctification. The seed, sun, soil, and water are given. But the preparation of the soil and the cultivation of the vine are necessary to produce wine. Wine is the product of the transaction between the Divine and the human, between nature that gives and human nature that transforms. Love, like wine, is a gift to be cultivated and tended with patience and purpose. Like wine, love is to be consecrated.

Another ancient Jewish wedding ritual calls for the bride and groom to each lift their respective cups of wine and pour a portion of the wine into an empty cup that symbolizes the emptiness of a world without love. Looking into the newly blended cup of wine, neither bride nor groom knows which is his or her contribution. They become as one. The mixing of the wine represents the merger of the lives of the groom and bride, whose combined love fills emptiness with meaning.

The Broken Glass

The closing ritual gesture at the wedding ceremony calls for the groom to break a glass placed beneath his foot. While it may appear to be a dissonant act at such a festive occasion, it is very much in keeping with the religious intent of the wedding ritual. The breaking of the glass, evoking the memory of the shattered Temple of old, reminds the bride and groom of the incompleteness in the contemporary world, of the existence of hunger and homelessness today that is not to be denied or forgotten. The shattered glass symbolizes the brokenness of the human condition and the duty of the couple, gifted by love, to enter the world and make whole that which is fragmented and to bind the abrasions of the wounded.

A Note on Divorce

The marriage union is not always seamless. Judaism is reality based, and the tradition acknowledges that there are times when incompatibilities may only be relieved by the writ of divorce (Deuteronomy 24:1).

Jewish tradition, fully aware of the tragedy of divorce, stresses the supreme importance of *sh'lom bayit,* "peace in the home." Two illustrations from the Bible and the rabbinic tradition illustrate that the concept of *sh'lom bayit,* peace in the home, is so central that God personally is involved in maintaining and preserving the marriage. To erase God's name is considered an act of blasphemy. Yet the Bible speaks of the permissible erasure of God's name in a ceremony in which a wife is suspected by her husband of adultery (Numbers 5:23). In this elaborate ritual, the wife was to drink water of bitterness to prove her innocence and allay the suspicion of her husband. This ordeal of jealousy, later annulled by the Rabbis, called for the writing of God's name on a parchment that is then immersed in the bitter waters and dissolved. The erasure of God's name, a serious transgression, is nevertheless permitted because it may bring peace between husband and wife (Jerusalem Talmud, *Sotah* 1:4, based on Numbers 5:12).

In another instance, God is even said to lie in order to promote tranquility and trust in the home. The biblical episode refers to God's appearance before Sarah, promising her a son at the advanced age of her and her husband Abraham. Sarah laughs in disbelief, saying, "Shall I have pleasure with my husband, my lord being old himself?" (Genesis 18:12). But in reporting her reply to Abraham, God alters the uncomplimentary reference to Abraham's advanced age. Instead, God reports that it was Sarah's age that provoked her laughter of disbelief. The Rabbis interpreted this inconsistency as God's attempt at avoiding discord between husband and wife. To attribute a lie to God for the sake of peace in the home underscores how important maintaining the marriage is in the Jewish tradition.

While divorce is permitted in the Bible, the Sages averred that when a divorce takes place "the very altar sheds tears" (Talmud, *Gittin* 90b). In divorce, the Image of God is severed from its marital companion. But the Image within each partner does not die in divorce. The Image within each survives the separation and plays an essential role in the aftermath of the dissolved union. For parents involved in divorce, it is especially important to be cognizant of the Image of God that remains intact in each of them.

A couple may divorce, but in so doing they do not divorce their children. By remembering to acknowledge the Image within each other, divorced parents can better tend to the divine Image in the child they have borne. Bar/bat mitzvah events have too often become occasions for acting out postdivorce enmity, wherein children are caught between the tugs of loyalty to both parents. Yet, some divorced parents have managed to put on a face of cordiality in the presence of the child, the family, friends, and the congregation. In one unforgettable instance, divorced parents who joined to receive the honor of an *aliyah* at their child's bat mitzvah recited the blessings, then turned toward each other and embraced. The wonderment on the face of the child and her first smile on the pulpit that day spoke volumes. The act of the parents was profoundly instructive. That embrace taught the child a number of significant family values. The child was taught that feelings must be respected, that shaming another in public is like shedding blood, that love costs and that pride can be swallowed, and that a gesture of reconciliation at that moment is an act of nobility. It did not reconcile the couple, but it helped bring parents and child closer together. The family found each other in Judaism. The child learned the meaning of the moral aphorism in our tradition: "Who is strong? One who can control one's impulses" (*Pirkei Avot* 4:1). In divorce, a shadow falls over the Image of God, but the spark is not extinguished.

A Ritual on Family Reconciliation

The reasons for estrangement of a family are not limited to divorce. The shadow of alienation can hover over a family: parents and children who do not speak to each other, siblings who avoid each other's presence, cousins who will not meet, husbands and wives who publicly keep up appearances but harbor hidden resentments, lives endured in silent anger.

And it is precisely around the rites of passage that the insult to the unity of the family is exacerbated. The absence of members of the family at occasions of family celebration and commemoration is deeply felt. Sons and daughters refuse to mourn together for parents, and rabbis are asked to officiate at separate unveilings. There is a muted cry for recognition and reconciliation that appeals to Jewish wisdom for help.

"All real life is meeting," Martin Buber averred. Here there is no dialogue and no life. There is no opportunity to find a "thou." You cannot say "thou" to yourself. How can we break through the silence? What resources are there in Judaism to point the way to reconciliation? The Days of Awe in particular are filled with a liturgy that calls for repair, for the binding up of the wounds we have inflicted on others and ourselves. These are the days when a mirror is held up to our inner souls, when we are reminded that the heart of our prayers is *t'shuvah,* the act of spiritual preparation and inner transformation. These are the days when the prayers insist that God forgives, that God pardons, that God seeks reconciliation. We need to ask ourselves, whom do you forgive, whom do you pardon, and with whom do you seek reconciliation? Or do you think that reconciliation is only God's affair, that forgiving and pardoning and appeasing runs only vertically, from up down or from down up, not horizontally side to side?

The tradition of the Sages anticipated the segregation of God from man, the tendency to treat prayer vertically and to dismiss its horizontal implication. The Talmud says that while for transgressions between God and the individual the Day of Atonement atones, for those transgressions between the individual and his or her fellow human being the Day of Atonement does not atone, unless one personally appeases the other and seeks forgiveness. If you ask for forgiveness from God, acknowledging your transgressions but confident that God forgives, how can you remain stiff, silent, and unforgiving with others? The vertical atonement between God and man may not circumvent the horizontal direction of prayer. Authentic prayer is no soliloquy; it leads to a dialogue with others. To be meaningful, prayer must translate us out of the seat in the sanctuary into our homes and our families.

It is said often enough, "How can I forget the hurt and humiliation?" But forgiveness has nothing to do with forgetfulness. No one and nothing in Judaism call for an act of willful amnesia. To forgive is not to forget. To forgive is to be liberated from the gnawing anger and the quest for vengeance that consume our life and embitter the life of the family. The requisite for reconciliation is not forgetfulness. No one expects that forgiveness will erase the memory of the anguish. No one expects that reconciliation will return the relationship to its original innocence. A rabbinic Sage suggested the following simile: Sin is like the pounding of nails into a wooden chest. And reconciliation is like the removal of those nails. The nails may be removed, but the holes remain. The holes are not eliminated, but the nails, which tear at the soul of your being and tear families apart, can be removed.

The confession liturgy throughout Yom Kippur suggests a ritual of reconciliation. The insistence of the ritual prayers asking forgiveness urges us to seize the sanctity of these days and break the blind impasse. The prayers do not end with the final hymn in the sanctuary. They are prologue to the initiation of the first call that breaks into the dark silence. They call us to gird our loins and take the first step, to utter the first word of beginning. They counsel us not to rehearse the alleged origins of the dispute but to declare simply, "I miss you. My children miss you. I do not want to visit our angers on our children and our children's children." These rituals present a model of a way we can find each other in Judaism. The Days of Awe offer a sacred opportunity to recover *sh'lom bayit,* the wholeness of the home, which can be replicated at any time in the year.

The moral theology underlying the Days of Awe calls for moral behavior. To seek reconciliation is to teach our children and other members of the family that prayer is serious and has consequences. The act of reconciliation demonstrates the efficacy of our spiritual convictions.

Meditations

✦ *Wine, Canopy, Ring, and Glass*

My cup of wine poured with thine
Into one empty vessel.
Drink a new mixture,
Our wines like our lives intermingled,
Fusion without coercion,
Merger without loss,
A curious admixture,
Two into one,
One into two,
Union without subtraction,
Singularity multiplied.

Four separate poles
Too close, the cover collapses,
Too far, it will not hold.
Let there be space in our togetherness,
Distance that holds together.

The ring unbejeweled,
Simple as love,
Not blinding our vision.
The ring,
A circle not to exclude
But to embrace.
An encirclement
Reaching for the hem of God.

The glass broken,
Symbol of fragility.
Strong we are
Yet vulnerable.
Gentle now, soft now, tender now.
We two are fragile
As the broken glass.

Love more powerful than death.
    Heals, binds, cures, cares, resurrects,
Sharing faith and fate
    Place and time.
    Seal the sacred friendship,
A new world created
A new beginning
A new promise.
Rejoice the world that rejoices us.

◆ *Yet (For Malkah)*

They say—we were not born together.
We come from different families, different schools, different associations.
    You are not me,
    And I am not you.

Yet—
    You know me better than I know myself.
    You complete my sentences, fill in the pauses,
    Read between my lines.

You are not me—and I am not you.
Yet when we are not together
My sight, my hearing, my touch are different.
The joys of nature, the amenities of life fade.

If you and I are not one,
Why then in your absence is my joy so dependent upon yours?
Why does your sadness throw me into despair?
Why is your ache mine?

We are separate.

Yet—
 You know me so well.
 In Hebrew love and knowledge are the same—*daat*
 To know is to love,
 To love is to know.

We are not the same.

Yet—
 You know me with the mind of the heart,
 My strengths and weaknesses,
 My dreams and angers.
You know me in the marrow of your being.

They say that five decades is a long time in marriage.

And yet—
 How brief it is.
 How much yet to grow,
 How much yet to discover about ourselves,
 Through each other.

We have reached—
 The harvest of many years.
 Children and children's children now,
 Dance and play before us,
 And in their eyes we see yet another part of ourselves.
 The best is yet to be.

✦ *A New Syntax*

"The whole world was created for the sake of marriage."
To unite the divided,
To bring together the separate.
A mysterious mathematics:
Two into one
One into two.

A self-discovery.
Through another to learn my interior self.
Not in solitary contemplation
But with another to whom I say thou,
With all my soul, mind, and might,
I am newly revealed.

Blessed the union that turns I, me, and mine
Into we, us, and ours.
Blessed this union that issues a new grammar of love.

◆ *The Deepest Choice*

A different chemistry in marriage;
Not I becoming you or you becoming me,
Not I absorbing you,
Or you absorbing me.
Without loss of identity,
An enlargement of each.

A union, not by coercion,
Not by surrender or domination,
But by choice.
Did not Ruth describe our bond?
"Where you go I will go,
Where you lodge I will lodge,
Your people shall be my people,
Your God my God."

Sharing faith and fate,
Place and time,
Be thou consecrated
Unto me.

✦ *The Glass Is Broken*

How at the height of joy
    Is a glass broken?
How in the midst of song
    Intrudes the noise of shattered glass?

A moment past the sacred vows,
    Open now to fragmented lives.
Bride and groom embracing time beyond,
    With the final promise to each other,
Carried beyond the four posts of the wedding canopy
    Into the blemished world.

✦ *Mirror Eyes*

The mirror is not neutral.
A cool, silver-covered surface
reflecting me impartially.
It has its own shape,
Its own concave, convex bent.
No two mirrors are alike.

Some mirrors make me look
Hard and gross.
However I fix my smile, it reflects
A grimace.
However wide I set my eyes,
It appears a squinting mean-ness.

Other mirrors see me differently
And raise me up to
New confidence, new trust.
No two mirrors are twins.
I choose one to find my own image.

Your eyes are mirrors.
And like them are not neutral.
In your eyes I find myself.
I choose eyes
Not focused on blemishes alone
But see that which compensates.

Not eyes that flutter flattery
Blind to flaws
But eyes that
Accept scars
As marks of suffering and growth.
Eyes that do not blink away my crooked nose
And twisted mouth
But wink encouragement and hope and love.

✦ *Meditation on Divorce: Broken Vows*

Once it was whole,
Vows engraved on two tablets of the heart,
Held in embracing arms.
Then fallen, dropped, cast down.
The letters flung out of the stone,
Left as a wordless rock.

Where to place the broken covenant?
Cast it aside like a broken slab?
Relegate it to cremated ashes?
Too much memory to be buried out of sight.
What to do with our brokenness?

Follow the wisdom of Moses;
Rise up, hew them anew, two new tablets
Different from the first,
Wiser, truer, hallowed by experience,
Like the prophet, set the shattered tablets
In an ark of holiness inextricably close to the new.

Sacred recollections of the broken heart, the clouded tear
Remind us that our children
Born of hope and love, God's fingerprints,
Are innocent.
Them we have not divorced;
From them we will never be separated;
They are ours.

As in the first wedding benediction:
Blessed are You who has made the human being
    in Your image, after Your likeness;
Let us vow not to shed over them our anguish,
Not cloud them in our sadness,
Not use their innocence to win small battles;
Not defeat them for our victories.

In the name of love that bore fruit
We will bite our lips, wipe our tears, hold in our sorrow,
In their presence
And for their sake.

Together we will rejoice them in their festivities,
Heighten in them the fire of new joys.
Together we will ascend the *bimah,*
    walk down the aisle,
Stand beside them before the Torah,
Under the canopy of their love.

They are our children;
Blood of our blood, flesh of our flesh,
    soul of our soul.
Blessings of tomorrow
Risen from the ashes of yesterday;
Resurrection of love out of premature death.

✦ *The Mitzvah of Reconciliation*

A rabbinic midrash tells of King Menashe
A king so evil that he placed a pagan idol in the Temple of the Lord.
When one day the king decided to seek *t'shuvah*
To turn his character around and to become a new person
the angels protested
Should a person this evil be able to repent and be forgiven?
They locked up all the windows and doors to heaven
So that the king's prayers could not reach God's ears.
What did God do?
God dug out a small hole beneath the throne of glory
So that the repentance of King Menashe could be heard.
God desires repentance and seeks reconciliation.

We who pray praise God
sometimes feel bored by the perpetual prayers of adulation.
We misunderstand the praise of God.
The purpose of prayer is not adulation, but imitation.
Not admiration of God, but emulation of God's ways.
To praise God is to praise the godliness within us.
Between us is a moral correlation.
As God is merciful, be thou merciful.
As God is compassionate, be thou compassionate.

We would be moved by prayer
But prayers are moving only when we are willing to move.
Bend the spine
Even as the shofar is bent.
Our dignity is in pliability,
our uprightness in conciliation.

Prayer costs.
Reconciliation costs.
Love costs.

The rabbinic term for prayer is *avodah,* "work."
Prayer that works must lead to work.
Prayers of reconciliation teach us to bend and twist and turn
To transform a self, a situation, a condition, a past.

Have we not biblical precedence for the power of reconciliation?
Mother Sarah and father Abraham cast out Hagar and her son
    Ishmael.
God played no favorites.
The same angel of God who stayed the outstretched hand of
    Abraham, holding the knife at Isaac's throat
Appeared before Hagar to protect her and bless her son Ishmael.

When Abraham expired, both his sons, Isaac and Ishmael,
Came to the funeral and together buried him in the cave of
    Machpelah.
It is father's funeral.
How will we honor his memory?
Will we continue to ignore each other and our common ancestry?
After the burial of Abraham
The Torah lists the names of the children and grandchildren of
    Ishmael.
They are family and their names will be read aloud in the synagogue
    to remind us of our kinship.

Jacob and Esau
Who was right?
Their parents, who played the dangerous game of favoritism?
Isaac, for loving Esau, Rebekah for loving Jacob?
But when Jacob and Esau met each other years later,
Esau ran to meet Jacob and embraced him,
Fell upon his neck and kissed him.
And the brothers both wept.
Who was right, Jacob or Esau?
What is important are not the disputations over the causes of our
    quarrels, but the consequences of our embrace.
What is important is not the memory of the origin of our conflict

But the deeper memory that we are children of the same father
And children out of the same womb.

Joseph and his brethren
The brothers who had sold him as a slave
Are now brought before him.
Joseph the vizier, Joseph second to Pharaoh
Now can realize a dream of vengeance
Cause them to grovel before him
Make them confess their infamy.

How shall the web of favoritism, collusion, and revenge be dissolved?
Joseph cannot refrain himself
"I am Joseph," he reveals himself.
"Does my father live?" he calls
And falls upon his brother Benjamin, weeping aloud.

Reconciliation is the denouement of the skein of betrayal
The unraveling of the strands of intrigue that ties the fringes of the
    family shawl into snarling knots.

At last, Jacob the father can wipe away his tears, stop his mourning.
Resume his prophecy as Israel.

Reconciliation is an act of moral heroism.
Our Sages said, "Who is the hero?
He who makes an enemy into a friend, an adversary into an ally.
Who is the hero in reconciliation?
He who opens the embittered heart and the lips held tight,
Who opens up the clenched fist and embraces the other with
    understanding."

The services are not over with the singing of *Adon Olam*.
The service begins when returning home we look at the mezuzah on
    the doorpost
And recall the inscribed fragments of the parchment.
"Love Adonai, your God with all your heart, with all your soul and
    with all your might.

Take these words to heart.

Teach them diligently to your children and recite them at home and
away, night and day.

Bind them as a sign upon your hand and as a reminder above your
eyes.

Inscribe them upon the doorposts of your homes and upon your
gates."

A proselyte is dearer to God than was Israel at Sinai, for the proselyte accepts Heaven's yoke without having witnessed the thunders . . . and trumpet blasts which attended the revelation.

Simeon B Lakish, Tanchuma, Lech Lecha, 5

4

RITES OF CONVERSION
Conversion to Judaism

We are a family, a growing family, which an increasing number of Americans not born or raised as Jews seek to join. This old-new rite of passage welcomes Jews-by-choice who seek to identify themselves with our community of faith. Given the increasing interest of spiritual seekers to become Jews-by-choice, conversion has taken on a life-cycle of its own. Through the act of conversion, the new Jew-by-choice becomes like one reborn, ready to be warmly welcomed and nurtured by the newly chosen community. Yet, there are voices who oppose opening the gates to non-Jewish spiritual seekers. They reflect the myth that proactive conversion that encourages non-Jews to become Jewish is contrary to the principles and practices of Judaism. The myth has cast a large shadow over the mitzvah of conversion.

Many have forgotten that the first Jew-by-choice was the founder of Judaism. Abram, himself descended from pagan ancestors, is mandated by God to get out of his native land and father's house. "I will make of you a great nation, and I will bless you. I will make your name great, and you shall be a blessing. I bless those who bless you and curse him that curses you; and all the families of the earth shall bless themselves by you" (Genesis 12:2–3).

Judaism's birth was through conversion. According to rabbinic tradition, Abram and Sarai seek converts, and through their missionary efforts, God became known as Sovereign of the earth as well as Sovereign of the heavens. Who was there for Abram and Sarai to make into a people except the pagan non-Jewish populous around them? Indeed, we are reminded at the Passover seder that in the beginning our ancestors were idolaters and slaves and that Passover celebrates the birth and the becoming of the Jewish people.

On the festival of Shavuot, which celebrates the revelation of the Law, the Rabbis selected the Book of Ruth to be read to the congregation. Ruth was a Moabite woman. According to the Torah, a Moabite was prohibited to be married to a Jew (Deuteronomy 23:4). But it is Ruth as proselyte who is remembered as the great-grandmother of King David, from whom the Messiah is to spring. The Rabbis proudly claimed others as Jews-by-choice: Bityah, the daughter of Pharaoh; Jethro, the father-in-law of Moses; Zipporah, the wife of Moses; and Shifrah and Puah, the Egyptian midwives who refused to obey the edict of Pharaoh to drown Jewish males and saved Jewish lives. We read in the Talmud (*P'sachim* 87b) that the exile of Jews from their homeland served to increase the number of converts, which is a glory to God. This sense of honor due to converts finds expression in the thirteenth benediction of the eighteen benedictions of the *Amidah,* which is recited daily. This is a prayer praising God for "righteous proselytes" *(geirei tzedek),* who are a blessing to us and to God.

How did the myth spread that Judaism is indifferent to or opposes conversion? The distinguished Jewish historian Salo Baron has pointed out that two thousand years ago Jews were ten percent of the Roman Empire and had increased their numbers from one hundred fifty thousand in 586 B.C.E. to eight million in the first century C.E. Conversion to Judaism was successful in those days and Jews worked hard to convert pagans as the Gospel of Matthew testifies when referring to Jewish proselytizers who travel over sea and land to make a single proselyte (Matthew 23:15). This historically documented proactive outreach to non-Jews was put to an end not because of the proscriptions of Judaism but because of the harsh edicts of the Roman emperors, especially Domitian and Hadrian, who considered Jewish proselytism a capital crime. In 313 C.E., under Constantine, who declared Christianity the state religion of Rome and declared that whoever joined "the nefarious sect" of Judaism would be burned alive. Such laws were incorporated in the Codex Theodosius. It was not Judaism that prohibited the proselytization of non-Jews, but the edicts of Hadrian forbidding Jews to circumcise non-Jews that silenced the proselytizers.

When the Jewish philosopher and codifier Maimonides was asked by

Obadiah whether he, as a convert to Judaism, could recite such prayers as "Our God and God of our fathers," Maimonides responded in this fashion: "By all means you should pray 'Our God and God of our fathers,' for in no respect is there a difference between us and you. Do not think little of your origin. If we trace our descent from Abraham, Isaac, and Jacob, your descent is from Him by whose words the world was created."

Sociologist Gary Tobin has recently appealed to the Jewish community, "Open the gates to all those who might choose to become Jews . . . opening the gates means embracing proactive conversion which is the open, positive, accessible, and joyful process of encouraging non-Jews to become Jews" (*Opening the Gates,* 1999). To those spiritual seekers who would enter the gates of Judaism, the synagogue should open its portals with joy and love. And in fact, since 1978, Reform Judaism has taken a proudly proactive stance toward conversion, encouraging the conversion of non-Jewish spouses and offering classes for individuals, couples, and families wanting to explore Judaism. The Reconstructionist Movement is equally connected to a philosophy of inclusiveness and outreach. The Conservative Movement adopts an accepting but not a program initiating conversion.

Jews-by-choice are to be viewed not as surrogates for our lagging birth rates or as making up for our Holocaust losses. They are to be seen as serious men and women who have searched their hearts and minds and chosen to attach themselves to our family. They contribute to the enhancement of our spiritual life and in turn are deepened through the wisdom and values of the tradition of our family.

The Talmud observes that the precept to understand and love the stranger in our midst refers to the proselyte. The Sages observed that such an imperative to love the stranger appears no less than thirty-six times throughout the Bible. The stranger in our midst is the mirror reflection of our own selves. A text in Leviticus 19:34 sums up the history, theology, and morality of embracing the proselyte: "The stranger who sojourns with you shall be with you as the home born, and you shall love him as yourself for you were strangers in the land of Egypt: I am the Lord your God."

Meditations

✦ *Embracing the Jew-by-Choice*

Our Sages have taught
You who come of your own accord into our family of faith
Are dearer to God than all the assembly of Israelites
Who stood before Mount Sinai.
For had they not witnessed
The thunder, lightning, quaking mountains
And the sounding of trumpets,
They would not have accepted the Torah.
But you saw no opening of the heavens
Heard no peals of thunder
Felt no earth moving beneath your feet.
You came of your own will
To trust in God,
To join our family
To become one with our fate and purpose.
To bind the wounds of the afflicted
And raise up the fallen.

Can anyone be dearer to God than this choosing person
Who has come to us knowing
The history of our oppression.
The residual forms of harassment in our own time.
The record of Inquisition and pogroms
Of concentration camps and crematoria.
Came to us without reservation.

We honor the courage of your heart and the compassion of your soul.
May you who enrich our family
In turn be blessed by us.

✦ *Ruth's Child*

With open arms we embrace
You, our Ruth
Trace your lineage to one who once taught us all
What it means to choose bravely.

"Where you go, I will go
Where you lodge, I will lodge
Your people shall be my people
And your God, my God
Where you die, I will die
And there will I be buried.
The Lord do so to me, and more also,
If aught but death part you and me."

Who are you?
Whose are you?
You daughter are bound to us
Belonging, believing, behaving
We are one family.
One God, one past, one present, one future, one people.

✦ *The Words of the Thirteenth Benediction
of the Weekday* Amidah

Let your tender mercies be stirred for the righteous.
The pious, the leaders of the House of Israel,
Devoted scholars and faithful proselytes.
Be merciful to us of the House of Israel.
Reward all who trust in You.
Cast our lot with those who are faithful to You.
May we never come to despair.
For our trust is in You.
Praised are You, *Adonai,* who sustains the righteous.

✦ *Discovering Judaism*

We have asked you
What you see in Judaism.
What in your classes of instruction and in your own experience
     has attracted you to this people
     and this faith?
You have answered and instructed us.

I have been drawn to Judaism for many reasons.
And in no order of importance.
     I have discovered the celebration of inquiry, the dignity of the
        question
     and the sadness over the fourth son
     who does not know how to ask.

I have found in Judaism the absence of dogma,
     apodictic authoritarian responses,
        answers that will tolerate no question.

I have been moved by the humility of the religious leaders
     who for all their erudition lay no claim to infallibility
        but know that they, like all who walk the face of the earth
        are errant souls.
No saints, unblemished but even as our patriarchs and priests
     flawed and fallible
     struggling spirits.

In Judaism I have found the enlarging embrace of inclusion.
No faith, no race, no ethnicity excluded from the circle of salvation.
No alien kept outside the circle, consigned to hell and perdition.
Not souls, I was taught, but lives are we mandated to save.

I am drawn to the faith that does not see sin inherited,
    an original stain on the heart of the newborn
        indelible sin that may not be erased by repentance, repayment,
        repair.

Injuries there are, not visited by ancestors upon our innocence
    but done to others and to ourselves
    which may be healed and made whole
    injuries for which I bear responsibility
    the capability to repair.

I am attracted to the inextricable bond between belief and behavior.
Faith demonstrated
    not with the declarations of my mouth.
    but with arms and legs.
Believing and behaving the twin duties of the heart.

In Judaism I find the focus on family,
    the matrix of human relationships
    mishpachah around which the community revolves.
Choosing faith I choose family
And in its history and literature I find my family album.

I find in Judaism my own inner self.
My choice of Judaism is not burial of my past
    but recovery of some hidden treasures within.
I have long felt its vague presence but never seen its face.
At long last, I have found the mirror that reflects the veiled,
    concealed soul.

✦ *Shehecheyanu: The Response of the* Beit Din

We accept you with love.
Not to supplant our depletion as a people
Nor to multiply our diminished numbers
Not to compensate for Holocaust losses
Nor gain another member in our world congregation.

We accept you
     out of respect for your earnest study
     your resolute conviction
     the decision of your own free will.

It is an honor to bring you under the wings of the *Sh'chinah*.
With reverence and joy we add your new Hebrew name
     into the names of our community.

Blessed are you who enter the covenant of Torah
     and the practice of good deeds.
Blessed are You, Creator of humanity,
     who has enabled us to witness this sacred moment
     in your life and in ours and in the life of God.
Baruch Atah Adonai Eloheinu melech olam
Shehecheyanu v'kiy'manu v'higiyanu lazman hazeh.

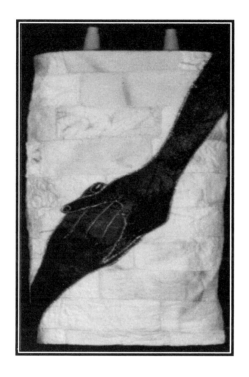

God created medicines out of the earth. Let not a discerning person reject them.

Apocrypha, Ben Sira 38:45

5

IN SICKNESS AND IN HEALTH
Physician, Patient, and Visitor

In one of the daily morning prayers we are directed to consider our corporeal nature, the ducts, tubes, apertures, and cavities of our own flesh. The prayer reads: "Blessed are You, who has formed the human being in wisdom and created in him a system of veins and arteries. It is well known before Your glorious throne that if one of these be opened or if one of these be closed, it would be impossible to exist in Your presence." The prayer may strike us as odd. What has this material body to do with the exalted spiritual notion of the Image of God within us?

A rabbinic midrash reports an exchange in the first century between Hillel the Elder and his disciples. Hillel takes leave of his disciples, who ask him, "Master, where are you going?" He answers, "To perform a religious duty, a mitzvah." Asked what kind of mitzvah he is about to perform, Hillel answers quite plainly, "I go to wash at the bathhouse." "Is this a mitzvah?" they ask in surprise. Hillel replies with a parable: "If the statues of kings that are erected in theaters and circuses are scoured and washed by the superintendent who is appointed to look after them and who thereby obtains his maintenance, how much more I who have been created in the Image and Likeness of God. As it is written: 'For in the Image of God made He man'" (*Vayikra Rabbah, B'har* 34:3). The body must be respected and cared for. Like the soul, the body is created by God. The two are interdependent. According to the medieval philosopher-physician Maimonides, the well-being of the soul can be obtained only after the well-being of the body has been secured. To care for the body, to seek medical care is an act of reverence. We do not "have" bodies. We are bodies. We live, suffer, and hope with our bodies as we do with our souls.

Not only must we intervene on behalf of our own physical well-being, but we are mandated to intervene whenever anyone is endangered. To do otherwise is to violate the injunction not to stand idly by the blood of your neighbor (Leviticus 19:16). A person who sees a neighbor drowning or mauled by beasts or attacked by robbers is duty-bound to save that person. (Talmud, *Sanhedrin* 73a). As co-workers with God in the completion of Creation, the human being is obligated to support the fallen, to loosen the bonds of the fettered, and to care for the sick.

The Physician

A revealing rabbinic discussion tells of two sages of the second century C.E., Rabbi Ishmael and Rabbi Akiva, who are met by a sick man who asks them how he can be cured. When they suggest that he seek out a physician for help, he challenges them. "Who afflicted me?" he asks. They respond, "The Holy One, blessed be He." The ill man continues: "And you interfere in a matter that is of no concern of yours? God afflicts, and you wish to heal?"

The Rabbis now turn to the man: "What is your vocation?" He answers, "I am a tiller of the soil. Here is the vine cutter in my hand." They ask, "But who created the vineyard?" He replies, "The Holy One, blessed be He." The Rabbis continue, "Do you interfere with the vineyard that is not yours? God created it, and you cut away its fruits." The ill man explains, "But were I not to go out and plow and till and fertilize and weed, the vineyard would not produce any fruit." The Rabbis explain the parable in this way: "Just as the tree if not weeded, fertilized, and plowed will not grow and bring forth its fruit, so it is with the human body. The fertilizer is the medicine, the tiller of the earth is the physician" (J. D. Eisenstein, *Otzar Midrashim*).

The exercise of human wisdom to take care of the physical self is deemed to be a religious obligation. Human beings are forbidden to endanger their bodies or to wound or injure themselves. The argument that it is their bodies and therefore of no concern to others is groundless. Our life is a reflection of God's attributes, and what we do to ourselves elevates or denigrates godliness in us. All things that might lead to danger must be dealt with promptly even on the Sabbath, because one must be more concerned about a possible danger to health and life than to a possible ritual prohibition. The Sages caution: "It is prohibited to live in a city in which there is no physician" (Talmud, *Sanhedrin* 17b; Maimonides, *Hilchot Deot* 4:23).

L'chayim: *To Lives*

The Sages maintain that one who visits the sick can cause him to live. Why is the visitation so important to the patient? Because pain, anxiety over disability, and fear of death and dying weaken the affirmation of life. Even though the visitation of the sick on the Sabbath may induce grief in the visitor, which is contrary to the joyous spirit of the Sabbath, *bikur cholim,* visiting the sick, is permitted on the Sabbath (*Shabbat* 12b). Visitation revives the spirit.

Recuperation requires the tactful presence of others to counter the hopelessness, lovelessness, and friendlessness that accompany illness. Curative forces are engaged in the body itself, but it is a conceit to think of a life as only a bio-system bounded by the outer skin. Family, friends, physicians, and nurses who tend to us with care affirm the grammatical wisdom embedded in the Hebrew term for life, *chayim,* which is written in the plural and literally means "lives." Life is plural. To circumscribe life to an isolated self is folly. The celebrated aphorism of Hillel that begins "If I am not for myself, who will be for me?" wisely ends "but if I am for myself alone, what am I?" (*Pirkei Avot* 1:14).

Martin Buber confessed that, in his youth, he preferred books to people. Books are easy to handle, easy to open and close, remove and shelve. He described books as manna from heaven, while humans are like hard brown bread on whose crust we break our teeth. As he grew older, though, Buber changed his mind and preferred people to books. "I knew nothing of books when I came forth from the womb of my mother, and I shall die without books; I shall die with another human hand in my own. I shall live with another human hand in my own" (*The Philosophy of Martin Buber,* 1967).

Once, the Talmud records, when Rabbi Yochanan fell ill, Rabbi Chanina went to visit him and said, "Give me your hand." Rabbi Yochanan gave him his hand and Rabbi Chanina raised it. The Rabbis ask why could Rabbi Yochanan not raise it himself? Rabbi Chanina answered, "The prisoner cannot free himself from jail" (Talmud, *B'rachot* 5b). The Sages claimed that the visitor of the sick removes one-sixtieth of the illness. Health requires the embracing hands of others. The Image of God within is uplifted by the presence of others in whom the Image of God resides. One Image raises another.

Hope, Morale, and Morality

The Jewish tradition is aware of the healing power implicit in the affirmation of life. This is dramatically illustrated by the following imaginative rabbinic interpretation of a biblical event. When King Hezekiah fell ill, God spoke to the prophet Isaiah: "Son of Amoz, go and tell the king: 'Set your affairs in order, for you are going to die. You will not live.'" King Hezekiah, hearing Isaiah's message, rose in anger and berated the prophet: "The way of the world is for a person who is visiting the sick to say, 'May heaven have mercy upon you.' And the physician continues to tell him to eat this, to drink that. Even when the physician realizes that his patient approaches death, he does not say, 'Arrange your affairs,' lest the patient's mind grow faint." This tradition of courage even in the sight of the angel of death comes to us from King David: "Even if a sharp sword is placed against the throat of man, let him not despair," Thus Job too declared: "Though He slay me, yet will I trust" (*Kohelet Rabbah* 25:6).

Who knows where the psyche ends and soma begins? Who knows how the spirit addresses the body? Life and health are sacred, and while there are times when acceptance and resignation may be in order, they should not be chosen prematurely. This stance has filtered down into a quaint Jewish folktale. It is told of Reb Moshe, a poor man who is gathering sticks for firewood in the forest. He places them in a torn sack, throws the sack over his bony shoulders, and then stumbles. The sticks scatter to the earth, and Reb Moshe, in despair, cries out, "Master of the universe, send the Angel of Death and take me from this earth." As if in response to his prayer, the Angel of Death appears out of nowhere. "You called for me?" Reb Moshe stammers in surprise and then says, "Yes, I called for you. Would you help me gather these sticks?"

Such folktales do not arise out of thin air. This spirit of life affirmation is drawn from the lessons of the Torah that are summed up in the penultimate chapter of Deuteronomy: ". . . I have set before you life and death, the blessing and the curse; therefore choose life, that you may live, you and your seed" (Deuteronomy 30:19). In praise of life, the Talmud says: "For a one-day-old child who is ill, the Sabbath may be violated. For a King David, deceased, it may not be desecrated" (Talmud, *Shabbat* 15b).

Hope should not die too far ahead of the sick. But hope is not the mindless optimism of Pollyanna that rejects any recognition of the gravity of sickness or any sobering counsel. Rather, hope is a measured wisdom that inclines us to basic trust over basic distrust. It is with such a melioristic stance that patients and loved ones are encouraged when confronting momentous decisions. At the end of the Creation story (Genesis 2:3), God ceased from all the work that "He had created to do." What is meant by the incomplete phrase "to do"? A homiletical commentary suggests that God created the world incomplete and that there is much left to do to improve it. To struggle to overcome illness, whether our own or in others, is an act of godliness in the ongoing process of Creation. It is a struggle that affirms life without denying the reality of sickness and death.

Meditations

+ *Facing Sickness*

My God I confess
I am no hero,
I own my share of fears.
Yet some things I need not fear.
I need not fear sickness as punishment
  Malediction thrust down upon me from above,
  Chastisement meant to correct transgression.
  Sickness as some test of character or will.
For these are not the ways of God.

My God in whom I trust
    Not an enemy
    Finding pleasure in suffering
    Joy in pain or fright.

My God I trust
    Through creative powers within me,
    Healing forces forming protective scars.

My God manifest
    Through unknown researchers,
    Physicians and nurses attending severed wounds,
    Helping recovery.

My God revealed
    Through family and friends,
    Prayers added to my own,
    Transfusing will.

My God
Within my tradition
My God whom I do not fear
    In whose goodness I trust.

✦ *A Morning Prayer*

Once I thought it strange,
    A morning prayer of gratitude for apertures, veins, and arteries,
    Now I have new regard, new wonder
    At the body and its intricate parts,
    A web of vessels, channels, pulses, rhythms.
A marvel of broken parts that can be sutured,
    Deep wounds congealing.

If but one of these openings be closed,
>One of the vessels shriveled,
>It would be impossible to exist.
I recite with new understanding the curious prayer,
>Blessed art Thou who heals all creatures and does wonders.

♦ *Playing with Three Strings*

Yitzhak Perlman
>Walks the stage with braces on both legs,
>On two crutches.

Takes his seat, unhinges the clasps on his legs,
>Tucking one leg back, extending the other,
>Laying down his crutches, placing the violin under his chin.

On one occasion one of his violin strings broke.
>The audience grew silent,
>the violinist did not leave the stage.
Signaling the maestro,
>The violinist played with intensity on only three strings.

With three strings he modulated, changed, and
>Recomposed the piece in his head
Retuned the strings to get different sounds,
>Turned them upward and downward.

The audience screamed delight,
>Applauded their appreciation.
Asked how he had accomplished this feat,
>The violinist answered
It is my task to make music with what remains.

A legacy mightier than a concert.
Make music with what remains.
> Complete the song left for us to sing,
> Play it out with heart, soul, and might
> With the remaining strength within us.

✦ *For the Visitors of the Sick*

> *This meditation was inspired by an eleventh-century author.*

Rabbi Eleazar Ben Yitzchak
Whose book of healing is called *The Ways of Life*
Is counsel to the visitors of the sick:

It is a mitzvah to visit the sick
The mitzvah is an art calling for tact and the wisdom of empathy,
A language that comforts without deceit,
Voice tones that elevate without exaggeration.

The mitzvah is for a sick person
More anxious and dependent than before,
More sensitive to the shape of face and body.

So do not sit on the patient's bed
For the *Sh'chinah* protects him,
Reminding us to honor and respect the Image that has not left.

Visit the sick, lighten their suffering,
Pray for them and leave,
Do not stay long, for you may afflict upon them additional discomfort,
When you visit the patient, enter with cheer.

I bring you prayerful greetings, my friend, from family and friends.
We have so much to say to each other, you have so much to tell us.
But if I part from you soon it is for your sake.
You need rest and quiet so that tomorrow
We may walk and talk and remember together.

I leave you joyful at the signs of your recovery,
Full of hope for the renewal of your energies,
Tomorrow we shall speak.
Tomorrow we shall laugh and sing.

✦ *May I Not Forget*

I have recovered.
    My heart full of gratitude.
I have recovered.
    I give thanks to the divine power
    In the skill of physicians
        The care of nurses
        The warmth of family
        Who held my hand in theirs.

May I not forget the goodness I experienced
    that I may render good to others.
May I not forget the healing power of
    friends, of good wishes,
      of prayers for my recovery.

May I not forget those long days and nights,
So that I may live out my resolve
    To uplift the fallen
    To help heal the sick
    To loosen the chains of the fettered.

I am a new creation
   understanding more deeply now
   I am more now than ever before.

✦ *On the Miracle of Recovery*

Menachem Mendel of Kotzk said,
   "Whoever believes in miracles is a fool.
   And whoever does not believe in miracles is an atheist."
We are neither fools nor apostates.

Three times daily in the midst of the *Amidah* prayer
   We acknowledge,
Rock and Shield that saves in every generation,
   Our souls that are given in God's tender care.
Three times daily we give thanks for the wonder, and the miracles
   that are daily
   With us evening, morn, and noon.

Surely we have read of miracles in days past,
In the turbulent waters on which Noah's ark navigated,
In the splitting of the sea in Moses' day,
In the falling of bread from the heaven that nourished our people
Forty years in the wilderness.

But miracles today? In our times?
Each day morning, noon, and night
Miracles in our time.
Where do we look for these in our ordinary lives?

Not in the violation of logic,
Of the laws of identity, and contradiction and excluded middle.
Not in the violation of nature,
Our wine is wine; our bread, bread; our water, water.

Yet in Hebrew miracle is *neis*—sign.
Sign, the root of "sign-ificance."
Sign, calling attention to ordinary moments,
Extraordinary in their transformation of our lives.

When illness threatens song and laughter,
Casting its shadow over our promise;
When inner turbulence, bleak and painful
Murders all hope;
When fear, gray, foreboding,
Contracts the surge of human spirit,
I pray:
Give me spine, heart, and wisdom.
Open my eyes to see wonder
    Open my ears to hear sounds,
    Inhale through my nostrils new fragrance.
    Walk with my own feet,
    Open my mouth with thanksgiving.
    Witness to every natural moment
    That raises me from melancholy to transcendence.

Blessed the godliness present in all things and ways.
Blessed the fortune that has enabled me to live in the midst of family,
    To reach this day in the presence of friends,
    With the benedictions of community.
Blessed the hidden miracles I daily uncover,
The renewal that helps me lift the stone from frightened heart.
Blessed the remembrance of yesterday's remission
    and tomorrow's promise.
Blessed the gifts we exchange with each other
    Morning, noon, and night.

✦ *Based on Psalm 77*

When I cry my voice trembles with fear
    When I call out it cracks with anger.

How can I greet the dawn with song
    when darkness eclipses the rising sun?

To whom shall I turn
    when the clouds of the present eclipse the rays of tomorrow?

Turn me around to yesterday
    that I may be consoled by its memories.

Were not the seas split asunder
    did we not once walk together through the waters to the dry side?

Did we not bless the
    bread that came forth from the heavens?

Did your voice not reach my ears
    and direct my wanderings?

The waters, the lightning, the thunder
    remind me of yesterday's triumphs.

Let the past offer proof of tomorrow
    let it be my comforter and guarantor.

I have been here before
    known the fright and found your companionship.

I enter the sanctuary again
    to await the echo of your promise.

✦ *May I Not Soon Forget: Postoperative Prayer*

Early in the dawn,
Before the bustling of the carts,
An old prayer
Flattened between commas
Resonates anew.

For opening the eyes of the blind
For releasing the bound
For raising up the bowed down
For redeeming the enslaved.

For straightening the spine
For supporting the faltering
For sustaining the weak
For strengthening the weary.

May I not soon forget
Lifted from gurney to bed,
The free motion of a tubeless body,
The first meal with teeth, tongue, and mouth.

May I not soon forget
The first lucidity,
The first cessation of pain,
The first walk,
The sweet fatigue of the first shower.

May I not soon forget
The vigil of families,
The wishes of friends,
The donors of blood and prayer,
The firm grip of doctors.

May I not soon forget
The farewell to corridor smells,
The triumphant return home,
The turn of the lock,
The loyalty of the mezuzah,
Standing watch in sunshine and in rain.

May I not soon forget
The Source of all healing
Hidden and overt miracles
Morning, noon, and night
Within me, between us.

There is one who sings the song of his own self, and in himself finds everything. Then there is the one who sings the song of his people and cleaves with a tender love to Israel. And there is one whose spirit is in all worlds, and with all of them does he join in his song. The song of the self, the song of one's people, the song of man, the song of this world—they all merge within him continually. And this song in its completeness and fullness, rises to become the song of holiness.

Abraham Isaac Kook, Orot HaKodesh II

6

DEATH, DYING, AND IMMORTALITY
Dying We Live

The Reality Principle

The cry "Why, why me!" arises from sorrow. It carries with it a set of assumptions, among them that from above, somehow, an otherwise just God has unfairly struck down perhaps ourselves, perhaps a beloved other, with a mortal illness. Death or the threat of death is converted into a moral judgment, a stance that has grave consequences for our understanding of God and God's imprint on us.

A number of the meditations in this section are based on a different understanding of the ways in which divinity is manifested around and within us. These meditations are attuned to the insights of some talmudic Sages who understood that nature is the creation of God but not God's judgment upon us.

These Sages believed that "the world pursues its own course" (Talmud, *Avodah Zarah* 54b). And they offer instances to demonstrate the neutral, amoral character of nature. So, they observe, if a man should steal a measure of wheat and sow it in his field, it would surely be right that the wheat should not grow. "But the world pursues its own course." Nature is not a court of justice. The earthquake is not juridical sentence. The tornado is not divine punishment. AIDS is no just dessert for the afflicted.

Nature is created by God, who, in the first chapter of Genesis, is exclusively referred to as *Elohim,* God, the power that creates the lion and the lamb, the scorpion and the deer. Those powers function amorally within the world of facts. *Elohim* is the Author of all that "is." We praise the heavens and the earth for the goodness of plenitude and beauty, not for its morality. Nature is amoral; aesthetics is not ethics. Nature pursues its own course.

But acceptance of the nature of things is far from the whole of the religious response. The more challenging aspect of the spiritual life involves the universe of the moral "ought." The human search for the moral normative calls upon another dimension of divinity and gives it the name *Adonai,* translated as Lord. Our relationship with *Elohim* provides us with the reality principle—that which is; our relationship with *Adonai* turns us toward the ideality principle—that which morally ought to be. *Elohim* and *Adonai* are one. The two are related to each other much as the realms of is and ought are related to each other. Acknowledging *Elohim,* we learn how and what to accept; recognizing *Adonai,* we learn how and what to transform. Oriented toward *Adonai,* we learn to call upon the powers within the *Tzelem,* the Image of God that may change, alter, and overcome the adversities. Oriented toward *Elohim,* we turn our attention to the nature of necessity, the causal laws over which we have little or no control.

Surely there are many things that limit the freedom and power and responsibility of the Image of God within us. "By force you were born and by force you will die" (*Pirkei Avot* 4:29). And yet, and yet. Victor Frankl, the founder of logotherapy, and survivor of the concentration camps, recalled prisoners who walked through the huts comforting others, sometimes giving away their last piece of bread. They were few in number, but they offered proof of possibility. Everything can be taken from a human being except choice. Frankl testifies that even in the hell of Auschwitz, there were choices to make. "Every day, every hour, offered the opportunity to make a decision . . . whether or not you would become the plaything of circumstance, renouncing freedom and dignity to become molded into the form of the typical inmate" (*Man's Search for Freedom,* 1962).

The world of nature and the world of morality are not warring adversaries. *Elohim* and *Adonai* are complementary dimensions of divinity. The nineteenth-century Italian rabbi and philosopher Elijah Ben Abraham Benamozegh contrasts the domain of nature with the domain of the human being. Whereas nature is a simple direct effect of God's creative act—what we have called *Elohim*—human action or *Adonai* is "the continuation, completion and in a sense perfecting of this act itself" (*Israel and Humanity,* 1995). The human being, whose powers of transformation are drawn from Adam's struggles, is "the redeemer of nature" (ibid.).

Elohim and *Adonai* are found side by side in the benedictions that surround the rites of passage, typically *Baruch Atah Adonai Eloheinu,* "Blessed art Thou, Adonai, our Elohim." When we confer blessings at the various rites of passage, we acknowledge the *Elohim* dimension, the givenness of the person who has reached this station in life, and the *Adonai* dimension wherein we recognize the transformative powers in the person. *Elohim* and *Adonai* reflect the dual religious responses of acceptance and transformation that run throughout the life cycle.

The Burial and the Image of God

The burial is to take place as soon as possible following death. Out of respect for the deceased, out of reverence for the Image of God, it is not to be delayed. This ritual tradition is based on a revealing interpretation of the biblical verse in Deuteronomy 21:22–23: "If a person has committed a sin worthy of death and he be put to death and you hang him on a tree, his body shall not remain all night upon the tree, but you shall bury him the same day, for he that is hanged is a reproach to God." Why a reproach to God? A powerful rabbinic parable explains: "There were once twin brothers identical in their appearance. One was appointed king, while the other became a brigand and was hanged. Now when people passed by and saw the brigand hanging, they exclaimed, 'The king is hanged'" (*Midrash Tannaim* on Deuteronomy 21:23). The parable views God and the human being as twins, connected souls. To denigrate a human being is to desecrate God, to deface a human being is to defame God, to shed the blood of a human being is a reproach to God. The Israeli novelist S. Agnon suggested that the Mourner's *Kaddish,* which calls for magnifying God's name, is recited not only to comfort the human bereaved but to console the divine Creator, for whom the loss of every human being diminishes His glory. God is a mourner at every death of God's creations.

The inherent dignity of the individual is comparable to that of the Torah Scroll. The death of an individual is like the burning of a Torah. In both instances, the witnesses to such events are required to rend their garments.

The disqualified Torah cannot be used and the deceased have no mitzvot, but both are buried and honored. According to a rabbinic insight, the broken tablets of the Law that Moses dropped were not discarded. The shattered tablets, which remind us of our failings, hold a place of honor in the Ark of Holiness beside the whole tablets of the Law. Such too is the enduring sanctity of the divine Image in life and death.

The Casket Is Closed and the Tallit Fringes Cut

With the same high regard for the deceased, the body is cleansed and prepared for the funeral, dressed in shrouds made of muslin, cotton, or linen, and wrapped in the *tallit* of the deceased, one of its fringes cut. During the funeral service, the casket remains closed. Public viewing of the body is discouraged. The casket is closed because we choose to recall the deceased in life as a *tzelem,* the Hebrew term for Image of God. In life, the deceased exercised freedom of will and bore responsibility for his or her actions. The deceased has lost that capacity and has become, in the parlance of the Sages, *Nireh v'eino roeh*—one who is seen but who cannot see (Talmud, *B'rachot* 10a). The casket is closed to prevent viewing the deceased as a cosmeticized object, an "it," and ourselves as voyeurs and spectators.

The ritual cutting of the fringes symbolizes the Jewish wisdom of letting go. The cutting of the fringe of the *tallit* invalidates its ritual use. The deceased have no further religious obligations. As the Psalmist declared, "The dead praise not the Lord, neither any that go down in silence; but we will bless the Lord this time forth and forever Hallelujah" (Psalm 115:17–18). The ritual invalidation, effected by cutting the fringes of the prayer shawl draped over the body of the deceased, is consistent with the Torah's struggle against necromancy, conjuring up the spirits of the dead for purposes of magically revealing the future or influencing the future of events (Leviticus 20:6; Deuteronomy 18:11). The ritual acts of letting go free the living from such fantasies and honors the spiritual part of the human being, not as ghostly, but as a child of God whose living memory informs our lives. The deceased can perform no religious duties, but we who survive are the surviving sanctifiers of life. We offer testimony to the immortality of influence of those remembered by fulfilling in our lives the ideals that the deceased articulated in their lives.

Another severance rite calls for the mourners to tear the cloth of their apparel. The ceremony is called *k'riah,* or "tearing," and is part of the process of the psychological separation from the deceased. Some scholars suggest that the tearing of the cloth allows mourners to give vent to their resentment, to permit the mourners' expression of anger against the shortened promise of life. At the funeral, the reality principle of letting go includes lowering the casket into the earth, recognizing the fragility of the human being, placing some earth on the casket, and reciting the biblical statement, "Dust thou art and unto dust thou shalt return" (Genesis 3:19). We let go in order to hold on.

The Ethics of Burial

In the absence of spiritual and moral rationale, rituals are frequently performed without spirit and meaning. A folk proverb observes: "Wisdom is often hidden under a ragged cloth." Asking questions helps ritual regain meaning. Why are so many rites surrounding the funeral austerely simple? Why the plainness of the casket, the dress of the deceased, even the discouragement of flowers? In a profoundly moving passage found in the Talmud (*Mo-eid Katan* 27b), the Sages remind us of the history of ritual customs and the ethics of mourning and of the funeral. In an early era, they explain, the expense of the burial was great, and the burial fell harder on the next of kin than his own death. So, the dead man's next of kin frequently abandoned the deceased. The kinsmen of the deceased fled, embarrassed. Rabban Gamliel came forward and, disregarding his own dignity, ordered that he be dressed in simple linen cloth instead of woolen, expensive vestments when the time came for his funeral. Thereafter, the people followed his lead to dress their deceased in modest linen clothing. As a result of Rabban Gamliel's example, a series of funeral reforms took place due to a desire to respect the poor.

Formerly, the rich would be brought out for burial on ornamental, tall, stately beds covered with rich coverlets, while the poor were placed on a plain bier, a box. The poor felt ashamed, and *mipnei kavodan shel aniyim,* "out of respect for the poor," the Rabbis instead insisted that all deceased should be buried in a plain box (ibid.).

Similarly, in earlier times, the face of the rich deceased was left uncovered, while the face of the poor deceased was covered, because the faces of the poor who lived in years of famine turned livid. The poor felt shamed to the point of abandoning the deceased, and therefore a tradition was instituted that everybody's face should be covered. This reform too was based on the reiterated principle "out of respect for the poor" (ibid.).

The mourning ritual embodies strong ethical lessons. Ostentatious funerals are not considered appropriate. Flowers at the funeral are discouraged, not as a principle of aesthetics, but of ethics. The memory of the deceased is enhanced when money that would purchase bowers of flowers is given to add fragrance to the life of the sick or the poor. We honor the dead by elevating the living. In death as in life, the ethics of the tradition instructs us to love mercy and to walk modestly with God.

Working out grief calls the mourner to recite the *Kaddish* for a period of eleven months. We hold on. But there is a limit set to mourning. To sit shivah beyond seven days or to recite *Kaddish* beyond eleven months is deemed excessive. And in excessive mourning, the Rabbis observe, one is no longer mourning for the deceased but for someone or something else, perhaps oneself. Holding on, we learn to let go.

Afterlife

What happens to the divine Image after death? It takes on other forms. The Image that in life is taught by word and deed is transformed into afterlife memories that shape the character of other Images whom the deceased affected. The belief in immortality suggests an analogy with the principle of the conservation of energy in physics. In physics, the total energy of an isolated system remains constant. Whatever internal changes may take place, energy disappears in one form and reappears in another. Similarly, spiritual energy does not disappear at death. It is transformed. What is remembered of the character and ideals of the deceased affects our way of thinking, feeling, and relating. There are resonances of a life lived and echoes of a voice that reverberate intergenerationally. Memory is not a passive retention of the past. Memory energizes our life and offers testimony to the immortality of influence. We are not alone, not even after death. Our immortality depends on the Image being remembered by others.

Belief in life after death does not deny the sting of death. Nor does belief in life after death necessarily entail belief in another place, or in another world. The Mourner's *Kaddish* makes no reference to another world. It refers to the world that is to be perfected and sanctified in God's name "during the days of your life and during the life of all the house of Israel." Strikingly, in the Mourner's *Kaddish* prayer there is not even a reference to death. The emphasis is on life, this place and this world. Life after death is a belief to be realized by those who, in living on, keep memory alive. Immortality is not merely believed as theory, it is behaved in practice. Life after death is in our hands in life. Whom we have influenced, influence others. The conservation of spiritual energy stored in memory has its enduring afterlife on earth.

What is to be done with the darkness that death brings? An ancient Jewish legend imagines the emotions of Adam on his first day on earth. At the end of the day, he noted the sinking of the sun and the spreading of shadows on the earth. Adam was convinced that the world was coming to an end. He threw himself down upon the earth, his hands spread out touching two stones. Upon one was written the Hebrew term *afeilah,* which means "darkness," and on the other stone was inscribed the Hebrew word *mavet,* meaning "death." He rubbed the two stones together, and out of its friction a spark was emitted, with which Adam lit a torch that illuminated the night.

In the morning, Adam awakened to observe that the sun had risen. He concluded, "This is the way of the world. The sun sets and rises." Created in God's Image, Adam went on with his life. Out of darkness and death, he lit a fire and breathed new life. Adam came to accept the reality of death and darkness as events that follow the course of nature. Death and darkness are not fate nor verdicts of a punitive God. Adam accepts both and comes to understand that sunrise and sunset are intertwined. He engages the stones of death and darkness with courage, and when out of the friction a spark is emitted, he lights a candle. Some rabbis speculate that Adam's first candle may be the origin for lighting the candle of multiple wicks at the *Havdalah* service at the end of the Sabbath and the beginning of a new week. At the *Havdalah* service, distinctions are noted between light and darkness, the holy and the not yet holy, the Sabbath and the week, polarities that must be kept from being polarized as warring opposites. Life and death, this world and the next world, life before and after death need not sunder our belief in the underlying oneness of all being.

Through the rites of passage, we celebrate the links of the great chain of being that unite our lives. Through the rites of passage, we follow the spiritual nexus from birth to immortality. Through the rites of passage, we are drawn together and to the intergenerational core of values that bind the family. Through the rites of passage, we are afforded sacred opportunities to find ourselves and each other in Judaism.

Meditations

✦ *Fear of Death*

Fear—not of death or dying, but of not having lived.
Fear—not of suffering, but of suffering for no cause.
Fear—not of extinction of life, but of having left no trace upon the
    earth.
Fear—not of finitude, but of being forgotten.
Take heart
    Make this a life not lived in vain.
Take heart
    Make this a life not lived for naught.

✦ *For Those Beloved Who Survive Me*

Mourn me not with tears, ashes, or sackcloth,
Nor dwell in darkness, sadness, or remorse.
Remember that I love you, and wish for you a life of song.
My immortality, if there be such for me, is not in tears, blame, or
    self-recrimination.
But in the joy you give to others, in raising the fallen
    and loosening the fetters of the bound.
In your loyalty to God's special children—the widow, the orphan,

the poor, the stranger in your gates, the weak—I take pride.
Torn are the fringes of the *tallit* placed on my body, for the dead
    cannot praise You, O Lord.
The dead have no mitzvot.
But your *tallit* is whole, and you are alive and alive you are called to
    mitzvot.
You can choose, you can act, you can transform the world.

My immortality is bound up with God's eternity, with God's
    justice, truth, and righteousness.
And that eternity is strengthened by your loyalty and your love.
Honor me with laughter and with goodness.
With these, the better part of me lives on beyond the grave.

✦ *The Shivah Candle Is Lit*

Closer to the grave
The nearness changes us.
Do we think we will live forever?
Speech, acts, gestures
that once enraged seem foolish now.

Before the images of shrouds
envies, jealousies,
sworn vindictiveness,
All shrivel into nonsense.

Before the shovel of dirt,
The sound of pebbles on the casket,
The angers and gnawing regrets
Are strangely petty.

How did the Rabbis put it?
At the end of time, when the Evil Impulse will be slain,
People will look at its corpse and wonder
That this small hill seemed so hard to climb,
That this impulse as thin as a hair was
So difficult to conquer.

Awareness of death may bring courage to live.
Knowing our mortality,
How dare we be afraid?
Before whom, and of what afraid?
Before what choices do we tremble?
What questions are we afraid to ask?
What doubts will we not seize with both hands?

The wise counseled
That each of us should live as if this day
Were our last.
And if it were, each breath would be deeper,
Each step firmer
Each dream bolder.
Standing in the shadow of death,
A brave new light shines.

✦ *Alone Together*

No one knows my grief,
Treasures my private memory.
I mourn alone.

The grief is my own.
Of my flesh and bone
I mourn alone.

But I mourn alone in the midst of my people,
In the minyan
With others who cry and remember
Their own loss.

Alone together,
An individual in community,
Present to each other,
We are each other's comfort.

Alone together
We are each other's consolation.
Alone we are mortal, together immortal,
A community does not die.

The *Kaddish* requires community.
A *Kaddish* must be answered.
A *Kaddish* calls for response.
Together we answer:
Y'hei sh'mei rabah m'vorach.

✦ *Eulogy for One Remembered*

Not the wisest
    Not the smartest
Not the kindest
    Not the most tactful
Not the richest
    Not the most successful
Not the tallest
    Not the bravest
But my own.

✦ *Bittersweet: In Memory of a Child*

Bittersweet
> The struggle to be born,
> To free the infant body from the womb,
> Sever the umbilical cord.

Bittersweet
> The first gasping for air,
> Listening to the heart beat,
> A life lived outside the body of another.

Bittersweet
> Hope revived out of ambiguous prognosis,
> Love clung to in the deepening anxiety.

Bittersweet
> The stilled body.
> Love never forgotten.
> Can the promise be resurrected?

Bittersweet
> May the memory of a life nearly lived,
> Help us look beyond the eclipse,
> Come to new light, new song, new hope.

✦ *It Is Less Distant Now:*
A Yahrzeit *Candle Lit at Home*

The *yahrzeit* candle is different
Announcing neither Sabbath nor Festival.
No benediction recited
No song sung
No psalm mandated.

Before this unlit candle
Without a quorum, I stand
Unstruck match in my hand.

It is less distant now
The remembrance ritual of parents deceased
I am older now
Closer to their age than before.
I am older now
Their aches in my body
Their white hairs beneath my shaved skin
Their wrinkles creased into my face.

It is less distant now
This ritual
Once made me think of them
Now makes me think of me.
Once it recalled relationships to them
Now I ponder my children's relationship to me.
Once I wondered what to remember of them
Now I ask what my children will remember of me
What smile, what grimace
What stories they will tell their children.

It is less distant now.
How will I be remembered?
How will I be mourned?
Will they come to the synagogue,
Light a candle
Recite the *Kaddish?*
It is less distant now.

Once *yahrzeit* was about parents deceased
Now it is of children alive.
Once it was about a distant past
Now it is about tomorrow.

✦ *Strange Envy*

Envy them,
Those who stand bent before the casket
    Wiping away their tears.
Envy them their memories of
    Warm embraces, gentle humor,
    Birthdays, anniversaries,
    Joyous meals around the Sabbath table.

Pity those who cannot cry
    Whose tears have long been
    Dried into resignation,
    Surrendering the promise.

Pity the dried-eyed sadness
    Of those who can only dream of that
    Which could have been, or should have been.

Pity those who regret what should have been said to them,
    Or what they should have spoken,
    The loves lost, the joys missed,
    The hopes abandoned.

Pity those whose memories turn on subjunctive moods—
"If only he had, if only she had, if only I had."

Envy the mourners
    Who with sweet-bitter nostalgia
    Slowly recite the *Kaddish.*

✦ *It Is Never Too Late*

The last word has not been spoken,
The last sentence has not been writ,
The final verdict is not in
>   It's never too late
>   To change my mind
>   My direction
>   To say "no" to the past
>   And "yes" to the future
>   To offer remorse
>   To ask and give forgiveness.

It is never too late
To start all over again
To feel again
To love again
To hope again.

It is never too late
To overcome despair
To turn sorrow into resolve
And pain into purpose.

It is never too late to alter my world
Not by magic incantations
Or manipulations of the cards
Or deciphering the stars.

But by opening myself
To curative forces buried within
To hidden energies
The powers of my self.

In sickness and in dying, it is never too late
Living, I teach
Dying, I teach
How to face pain and fear
Others observe me, children, adults,
Students of life and death
Learn from my bearing, my posture,
My philosophy.

It is never too late—
Some word of mine,
Some touch, some caress may be remembered
Some gesture may play a role beyond the last
Movement of my head and hand.

Write it on my epitaph
That my loved ones be consoled
It is never too late.

✦ Elohim-Adonai

*"Blessed art Thou, O Lord our God, Ruler of the universe,
whose strength and might fill the world."*

Elohim in the creation of day and night
Light and darkness
Lion and lamb
Insects and bacteria.
Revealing power in the hawks above the earth
In great sea monsters below.
In every living creature that creeps on the firmament.

Through the eyes of *Elohim*
It is very good
All existence is very good.

Elohim, God of omnipotence, before whom we stand, like Job,
To face our own impotence.
Out of the whirlwind, truth:
>Who laid the cornerstones of earth?
>Who shut up the sea with doors when it broke forth and issued
>>out of the womb?
>Who caused it to rain on a land where no man is,
>On the wilderness, wherein there is not man?
>Canst thou bind the chain of the Pleiades or loose the bands of
>>Orion?
>Do you know the ordinances of the heavens?
>Can you number the clouds by wisdom?

Elohim, God of omniscience, before whom we recognize our own
>ignorance,
Elohim, before whom we bow our heads and bend our knees,
The sovereign God whose power and reality we accept.

But *Adonai* is the Lord of all that ought to be.
Alongside *Elohim* is *Adonai.*
Adonai in the yearning and behavior of God's human creation
>For justice,
>For fairness,
>For peace,
>For harmony.
Adonai in the vision of a compassionate society.
Adonai in the transformation of chaos and violence and void,
>Into order, sanity, and love.

Adonai in the mending of the universe,
>The repair of the world,
>The binding of bruises,
>The gathering of fragmented sparks buried in the husks of the
>>world.

Adonai in the discovery of the self created in the Image of *Adonai-Elohim,*
>The Lord God, who breathed into
>Our nostrils and made us a living soul.

Elohim-Adonai,
Acceptance and transformation,
>The reality of what is, the reality of what ought to be,
>The reality of what is yet to be.

Hear, O Israel, the Lord our God, the Lord is One.

✦ Elohim *and* Adonai: *Genesis 1 and Genesis 2*

Two names, one God,
side by side.

Two names
Interdependent,
Each with its own nature,
Complementary.

Elohim at the beginning.
Out of chaos and void,
Heaven and earth,
The fish below, the birds in the air.
Elohim, ground of all creation,
Lion and lamb
Eagle and dove
And all the ways of the earth.

"No shrub of the field was yet in
The earth, and no herb of the field had
Yet sprung up, for the Lord God had not
Caused it to rain upon the earth, and
There was not a man to till the ground."

Adam and Eve.
The breath of life into their nostrils.
Dust into living souls.
Adonai.

The rain fell.
Plants and trees appeared.
Where before there was not shrub or herb of the field,
Gardens sprang to life.
Trees pleasant to the sight
And fruits for food.

Bless creation.
The transaction of human and non-human nature,
Kiddush and *Motzi.*
Not the grape on the vine,
But the wine in the cup.
Not the wheat of the field,
But the bread on the table.

Bless one God and Lord,
Thanksgiving to *Elohim,* the ground of all that is.
Thanksgiving to *Adonai,* the source of all that ought to be.
To *Elohim* for seed and soil and sun.
To *Adonai* for the seeding, weeding, threshing of the grain.

Accept and transform.
Create and appreciate.
Elohim and *Adonai,*
Creative harmony we pray to dwell in us.

Two aspects, one God,
Two reflections of unity in our body-soul.
Make it whole
Make it balanced
Make it one.
Blessed art Thou, *Adonai-Elohim,*
Who has created me in Your Image.

✦ *Between*

God.

>Where?
>Not in me nor in you.
>But between us.

God.

>Not me or mine,
>Nor you or yours,
>But ours.

God.

>Known.
>Not in isolation,
>But in relationship.

God.

>Covenanted.
>Sacred claims, obligations, commandments,
>Above, below, between.
>Healing, binding, saving,
>Redeeming, shielding, nurturing.
>Godliness.

✦ *Past and Future*

Death and dying: two words in ordinary language,
An abstract noun and a present participle.
"Death: a permanent cessation of all vital functions."
"Dying: the cause or occasion of loss of life."
> How concise is the dictionary!
> How exact its definitions!

But death for us is a mixture of moods,
Tears, salt of self-pity, brine of resentment,
Anguish over things that never will be again
Regret over things that could have been
Bittersweet nostalgia
Remembrance of that gray day,
A tear in the cloth, a handful of earth.

And now this moment
When together we cling to courage,
We who have the right to mourn.
> It is the dignity of the soul
> To hold on to the past
> It is the dignity of the spirit
> To take hold of the future.

To love and to forgive
Others and ourselves.
To rise from grief,
To sew the torn garment,
To live, to love, to laugh,
> And to remember
> Always to remember.

✦ *Holding On and Letting Go*

Hold on and let go.
On the surface of things
  contradictory counsel.
But one does not negate the other.
The two are complementary, dialectical
  two sides of one coin.

Hold on—death is not the final word
The grave no oblivion.
Hold on in *Kaddish, yahrzeit, Yizkor.*
No gesture, no kindness, no smile
  evaporates—
Every kindness, every embrace
  has its afterlife
  in our minds, our hearts, our hands.

Hold on and let go.
Sever the fringes of the *tallit* of the deceased
  the knot that binds us to the past.

Hold on
Not enslaving memory that sells the future
  to the past
   nor recollection that makes us passive,
   listless, resigned.
But memory that releases us
  for new life.

Lower the casket, the closure meant
  to open again the world
  of new possibilities.

Return the dust to the earth
  not to bury hope
  but to resurrect the will to live.

Artists, aerialists
    on a swinging trapeze
    letting go one ring to catch another
    to climb to higher heights.

Hold on and let go
    a courageous duality
    that endows our life
    with meaning.

Neither denying the past
    nor foreclosing the future.

The flow of life
    the divine process
    gives and takes
    retains and creates.

Old and new, yesterday and tomorrow
    both in one embrace.

The Lord giveth and the Lord taketh
Blessed be the name of the Lord.

✦ *The* Yahrzeit *Glass*

The wick in the wax that fills the glass is lit
    in silence I observe
    each flicker a flashback to a
    recalled gesture.

And at the end of the day
After wax is cleansed,
    washed out, the plain glass remains.

I recall my grandfather
    drinking hot tea from that very glass
    a spoon in the glass
    to prevent it from cracking from the heat.

The glass will find its place
    on the shelves of glasses
    indistinguishable from the others.

Using that glass becomes a sacred act
Holiness is not outside the
    cupboard of ordinary life.

The sacred is not in some
    other-worldly precinct,
    deposited in some shrine.

Here glass that once contained wax
    in memory of the deceased
    now holds tea and milk and coffee
    held to the lips
    its contents
    swallowed, absorbed.

What loving memory
    to know that my beloved continues
    to nurture me posthumously,
    a love that outlives yesterday.

✦ *Consolation*

I would comfort you, dear friend
Wipe away your tears
Turn your sorrow into joy.

I would console you
With words of ancient wisdom
Of the need for acceptance of the inevitable
The inexorable course of life.

I would speak to you of
The immortality of influence
The afterlife of memory
The echo of goodness
In the cavern of our lives.

Yet the Sages caution
Not in haste
To console the bereaved
Not too soon
To begin the healing.

I would raise the heavy weight
From your heart,
Wave a wand and transform your grief.

But the heart has its own wisdom
Sets its own time
And will not be rushed.

Now is the time for silence
The dumb silence that awaits
The coming of a new mood,
And a brighter spirit
With you, friend,
I will be silent
Tomorrow we will speak.

EPILOGUE

Surveying the contemporary Jewish scene there is evidence of a growing divide between the public domain *(r'shut harabim)* and the private domain *(r'shut ha-yachid),* between the synagogue and the home. Aside from the attenuating synagogue affiliation and attendance, there are signs of a growing compartmentalization of the cultural agenda of each domain. The cultural agenda of the synagogue is communal, its liturgy is plural: Our God and God of our ancestors, heal us, protect us, save us. "Judaism," the historian Heinrich Graetz averred, "is not a religion for the individual, but for the community. The promises and rewards attached to the fulfillment of the commandments do not refer to the individual but to the entire people" (*The Structure of Jewish History,* 1975). The rabbinic counsel offered the individual is not to separate oneself from the community (*Pirkei Avot* 2:5).

But the interests and demands of the private domain are not always those of the public agenda. Increasingly one hears the individual counter, "Do not tell me what I can do for the synagogue; tell me what the synagogue can do for me. Do not tell me what I can do for Judaism. Tell me what Judaism can do to strengthen my family, to deal with the disharmonies of marriage, to heal the rift between the generations, to correct the aimlessness of my ambitions."

The disparate interests in culture of the public sanctuary and the private home has rent in two the wisdom of Hillel's rhetorical questions: "If I am not for myself, who will be for me? But if I am for myself alone, what am

I?" (*Pirkei Avot* 1:14). Hillel's complementary aphorism calls for the integration of self and community. That healing of the growing division between the two domains is a major challenge for reuniting the spiritual life. The private-public rites of passage are promising areas for the renewal of attenuated relationships. The poetry, philosophy, and ethics commemorating life passages can help breach the chasm between the private and public complementary cultures. The rites of passage may bring the concerns of the self and family closer to the enlargement of the communal vision and to the mutual enrichment of each. It is in the rites of passage that "I" and "we" meet.